631ART.COM PRESENTS :

"COSMIC INSPIRATION"

A COLORING BOOK

BY EDDIE ALFARO

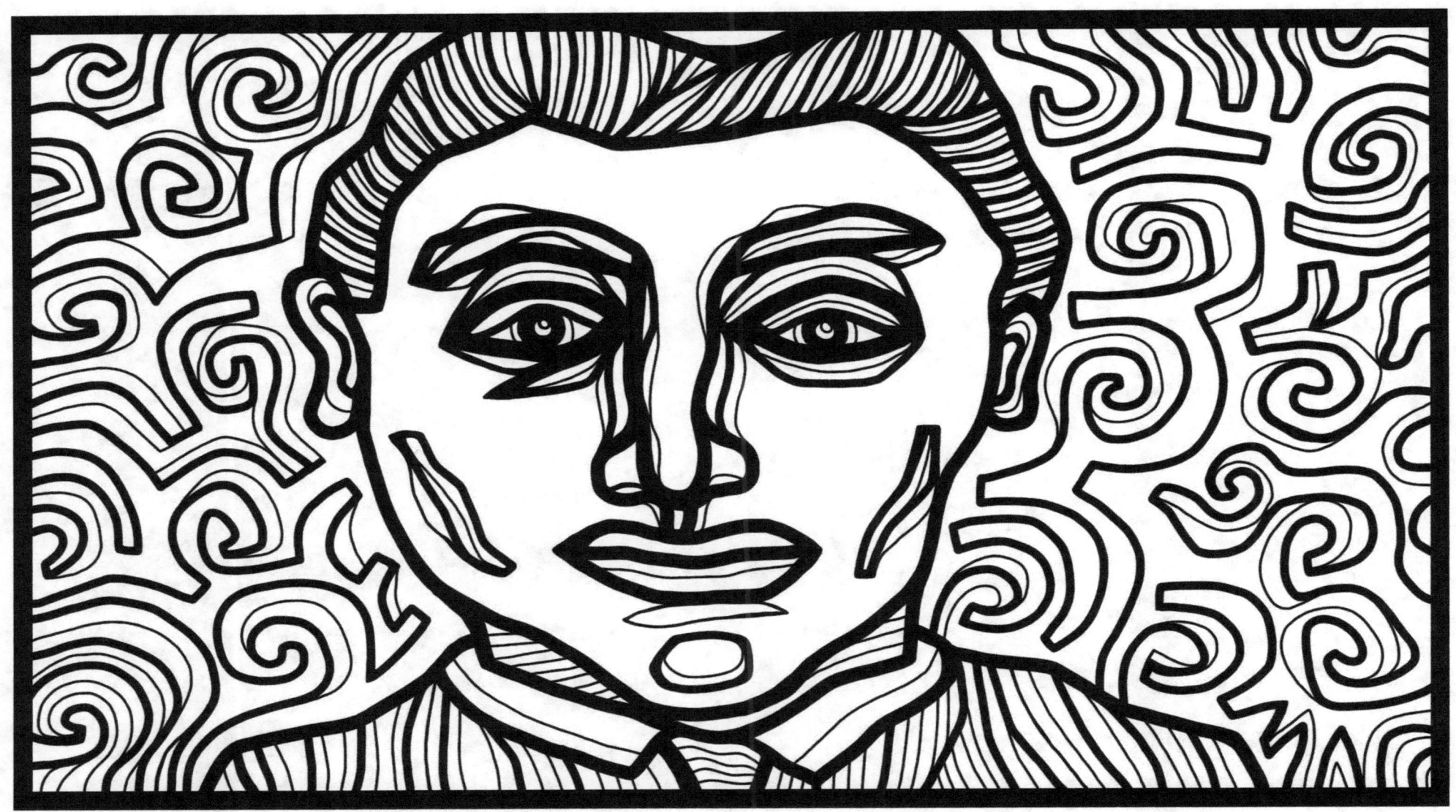

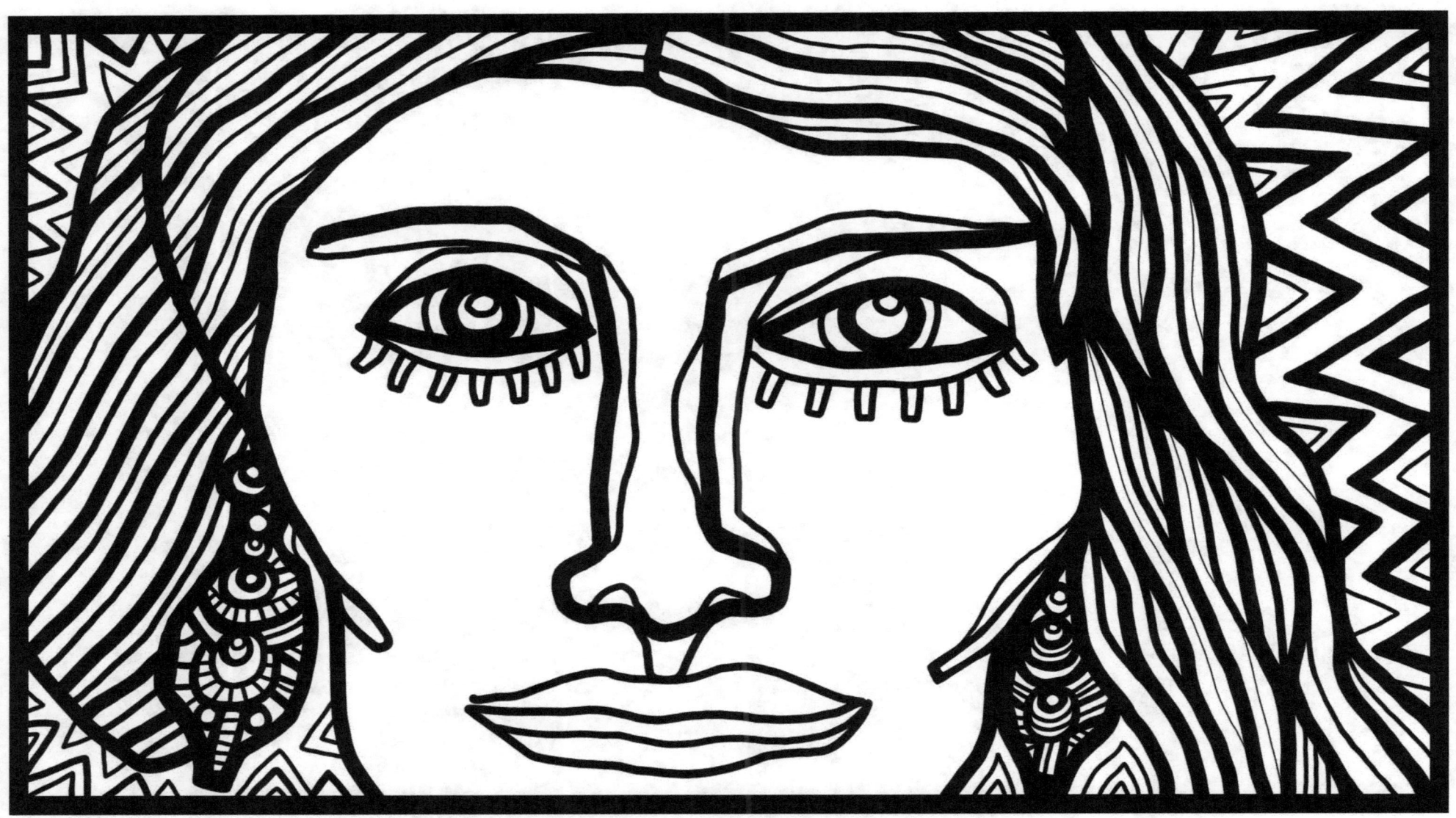

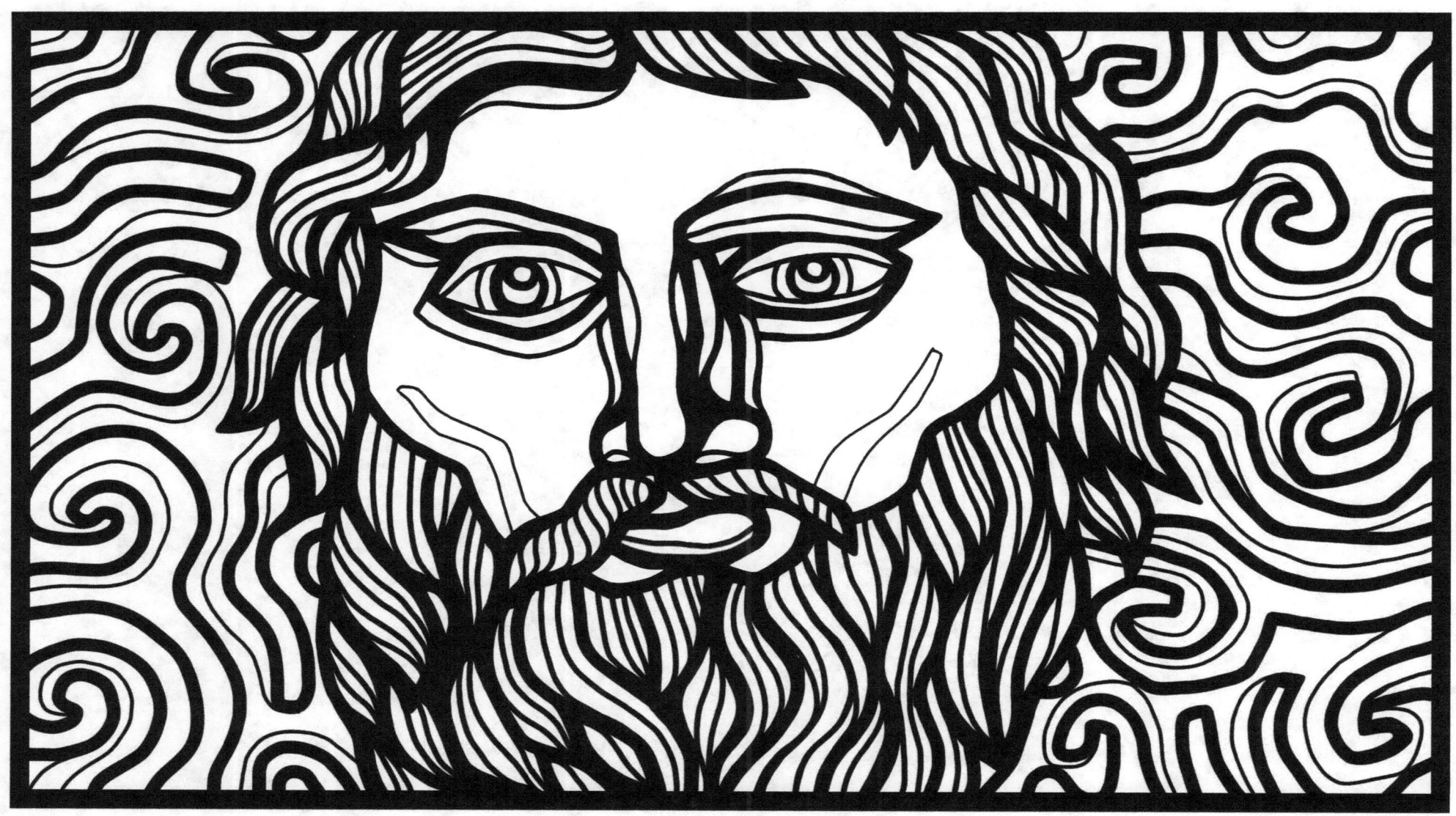

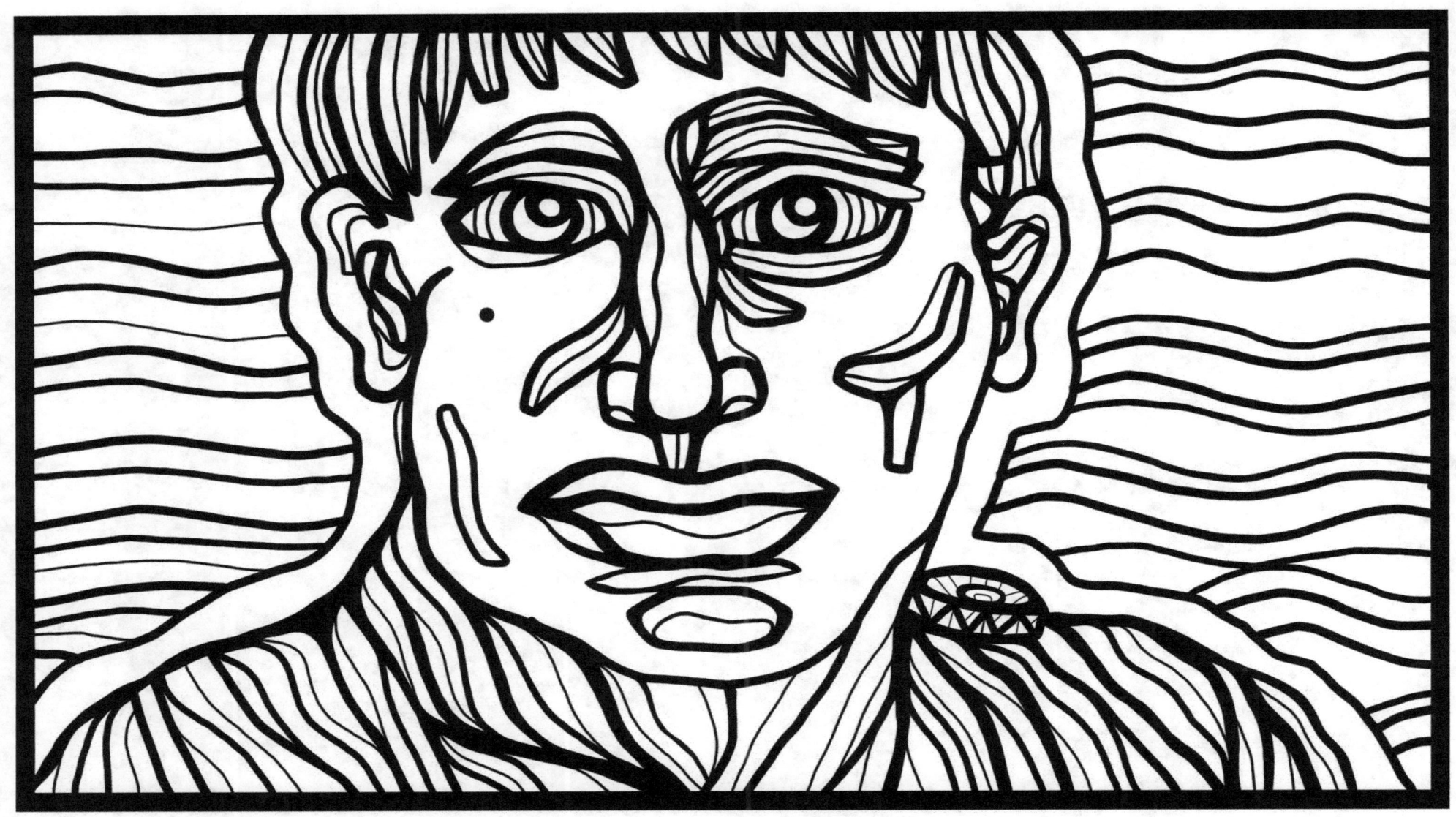

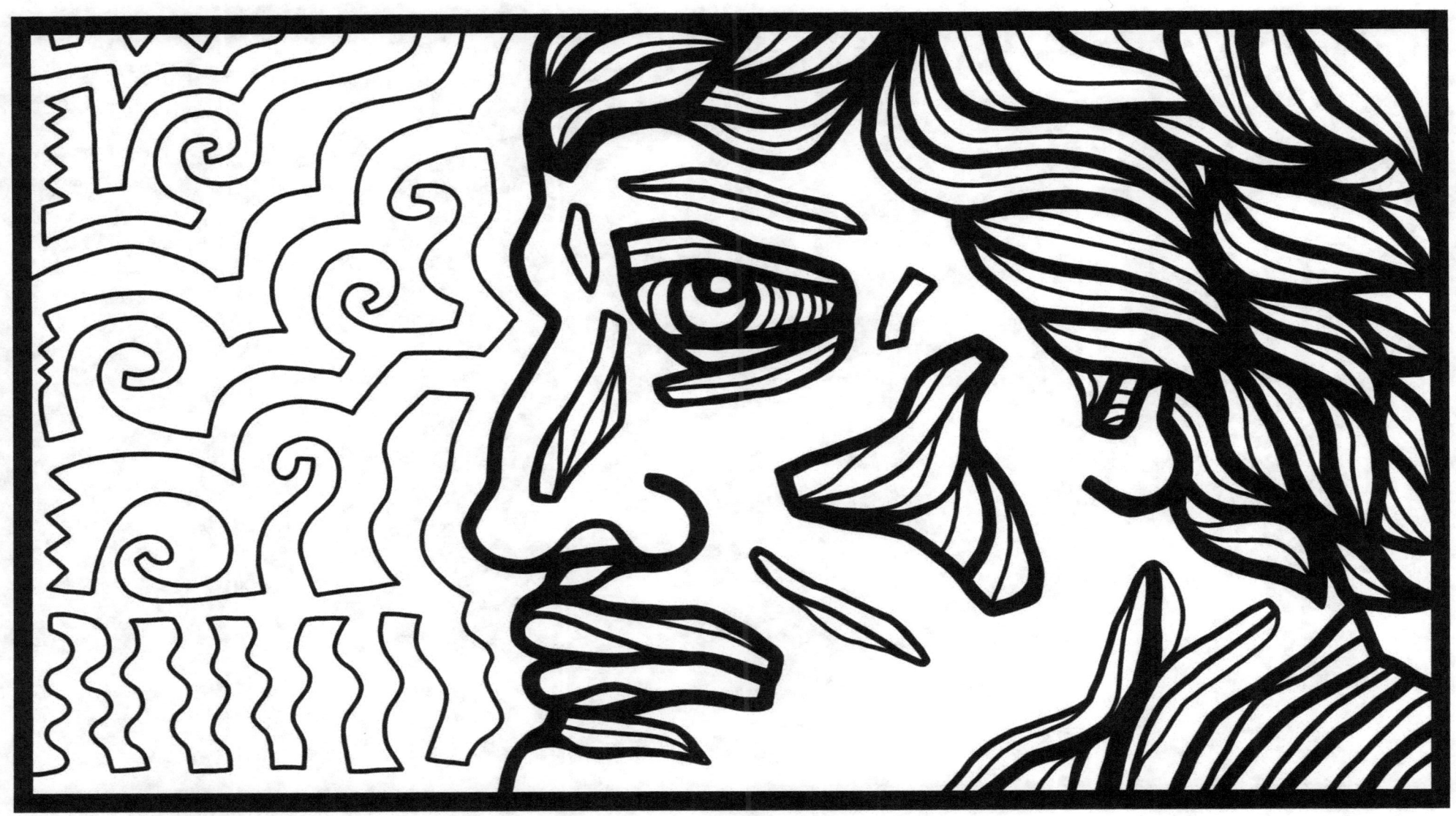

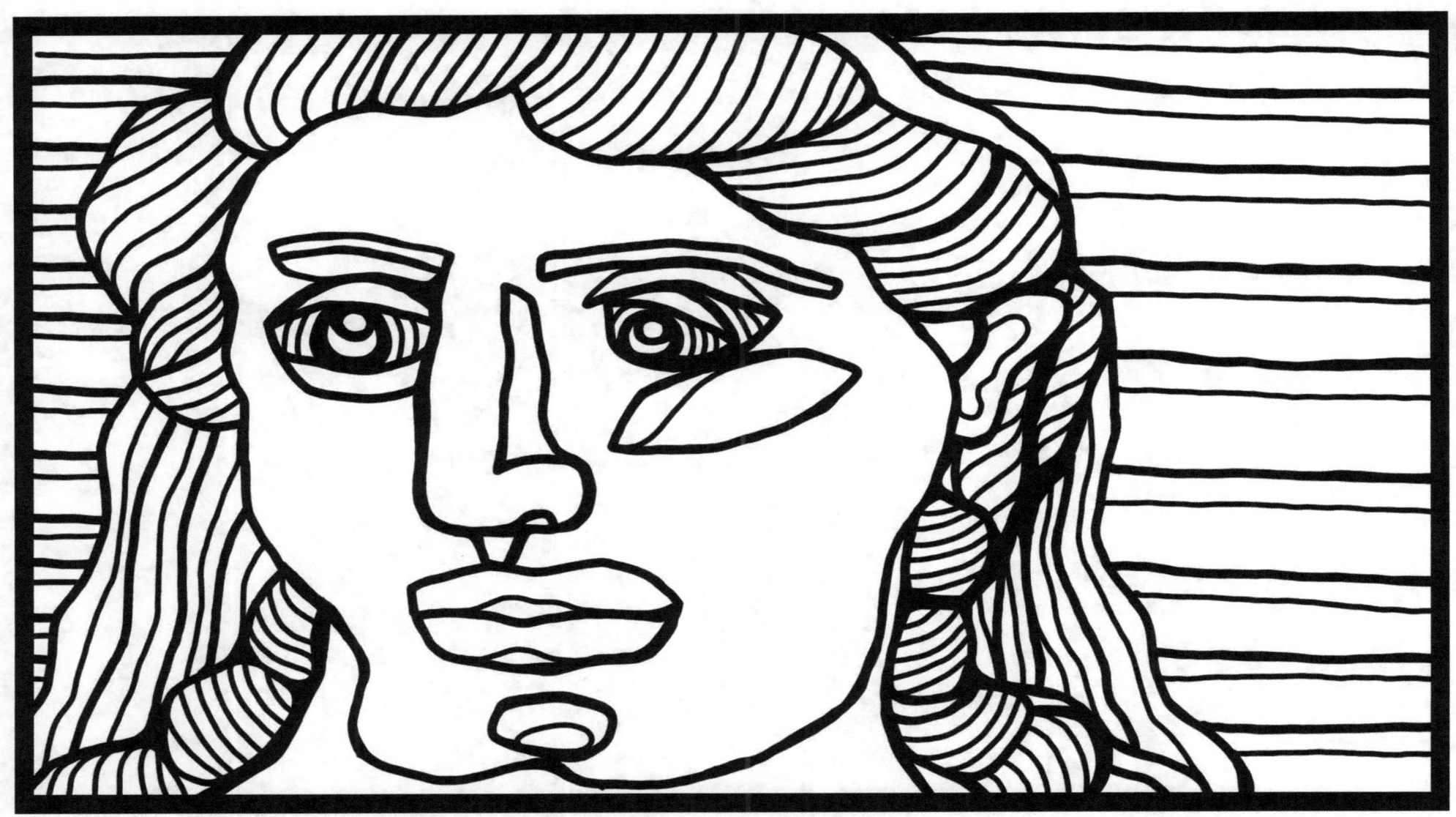

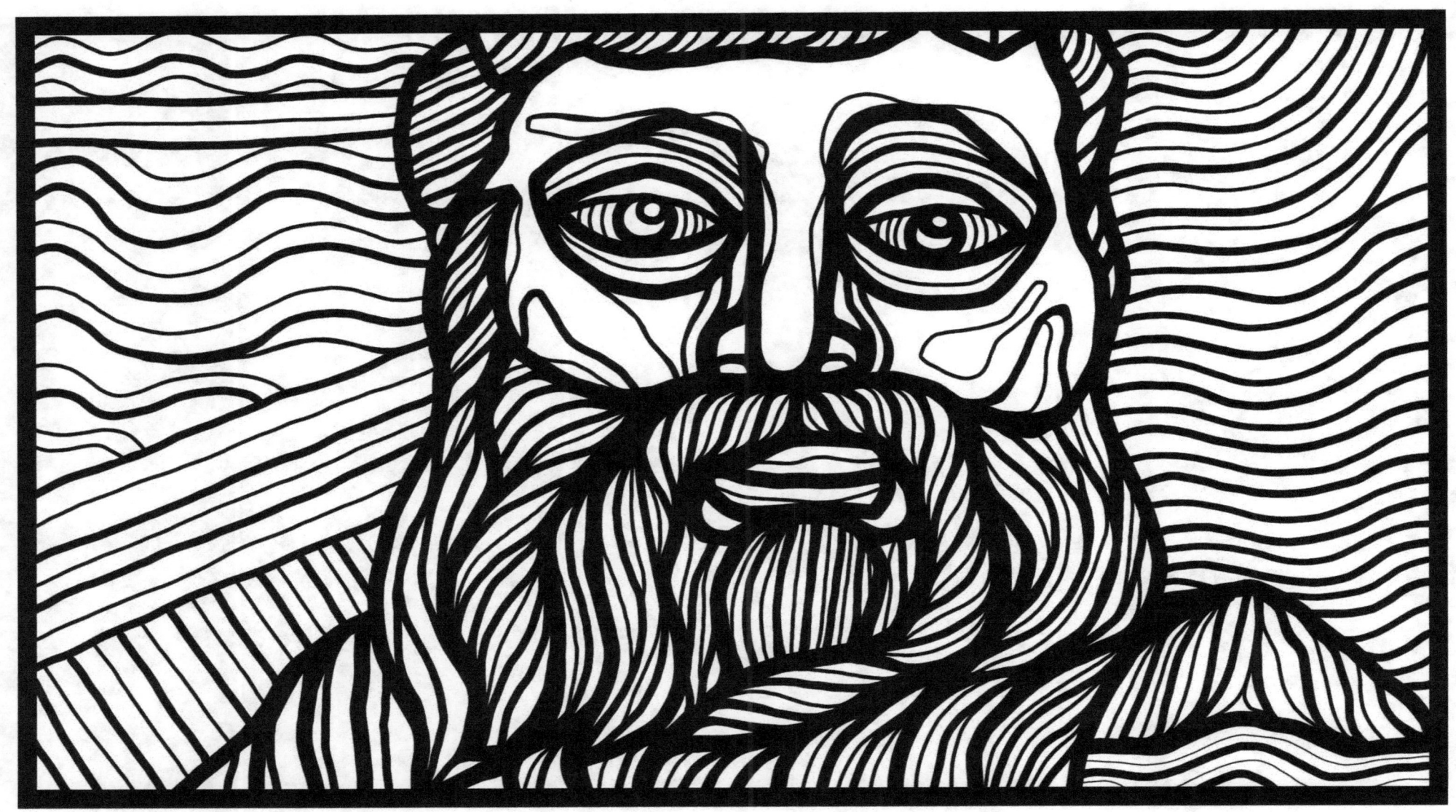

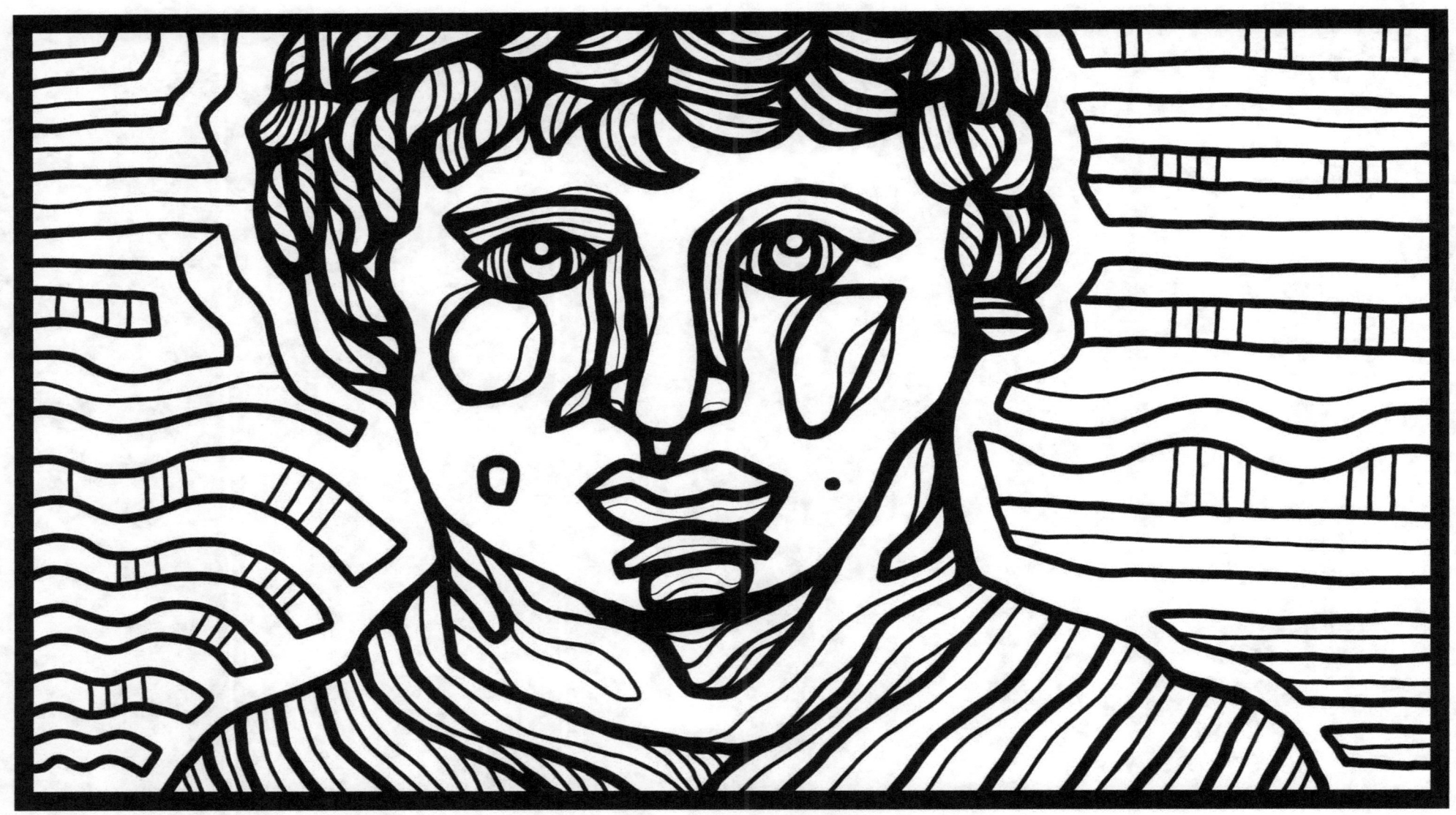

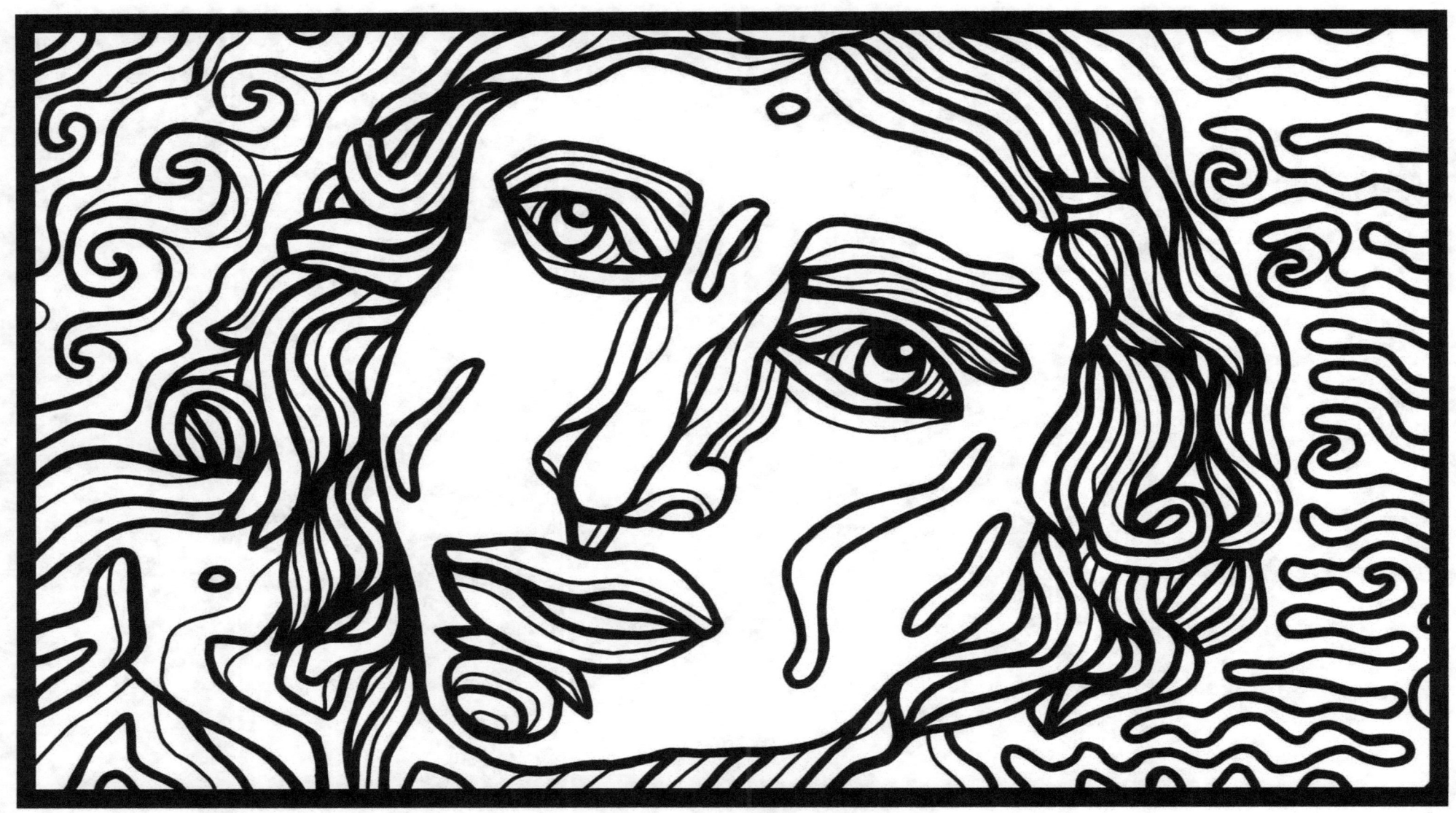

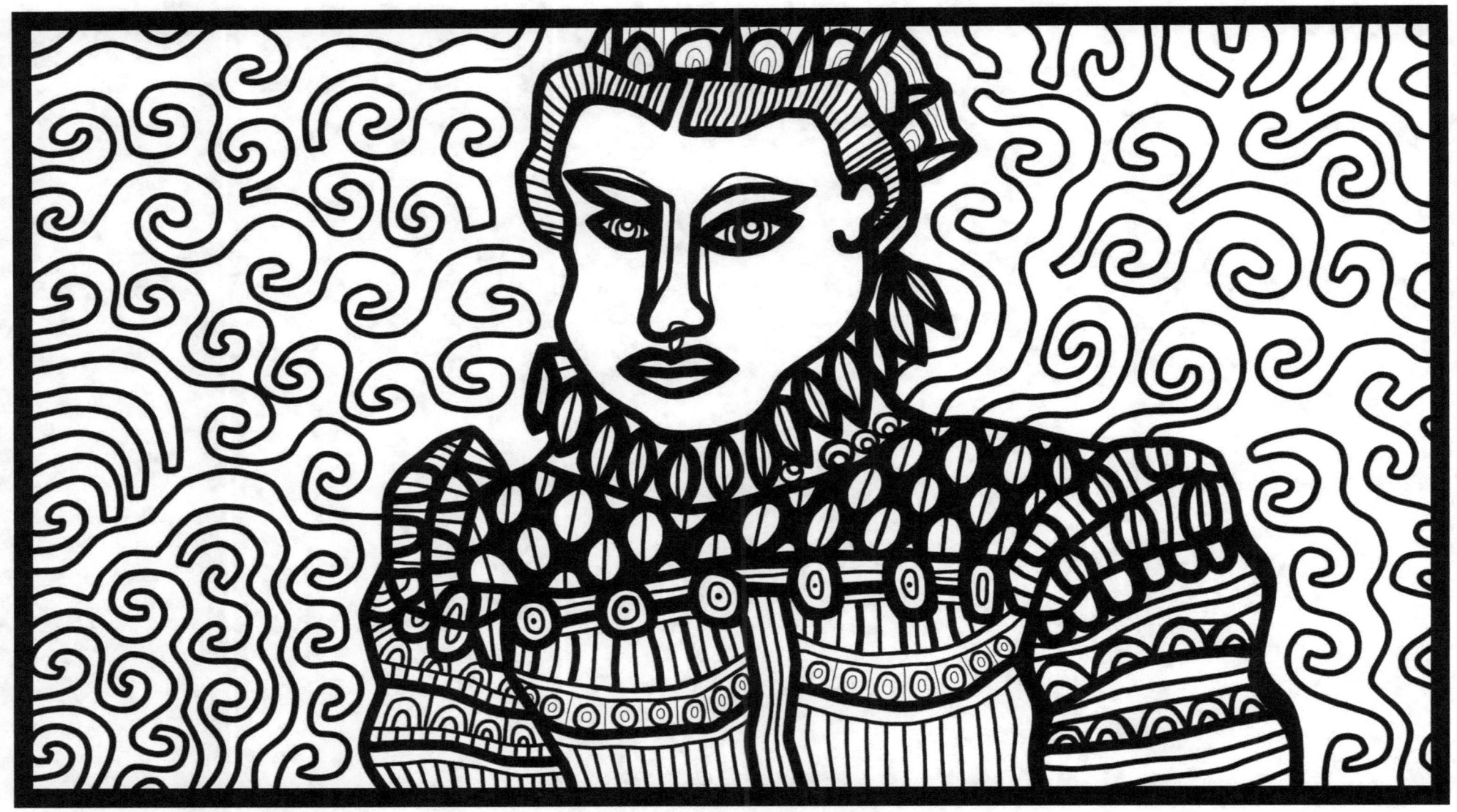

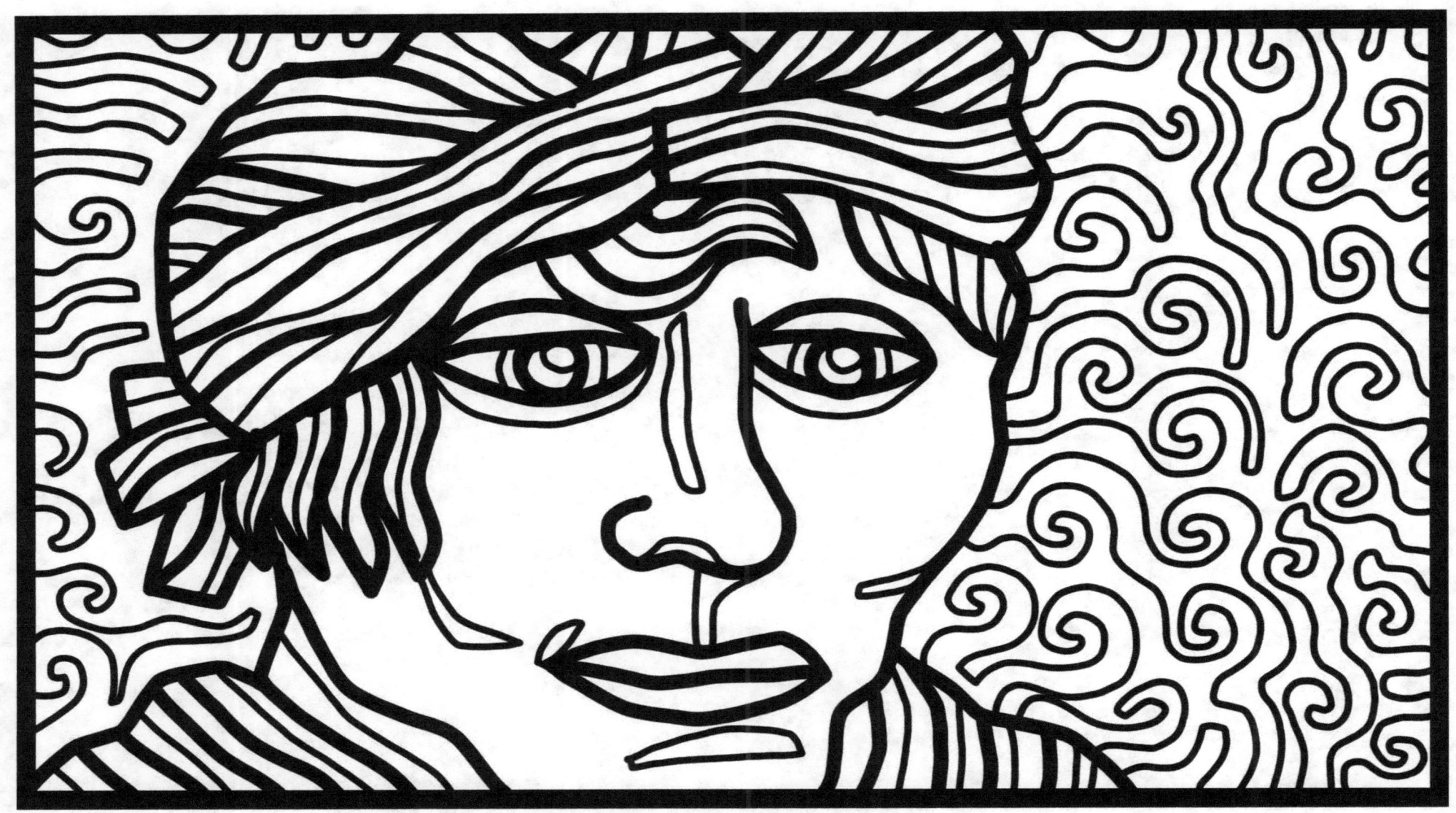

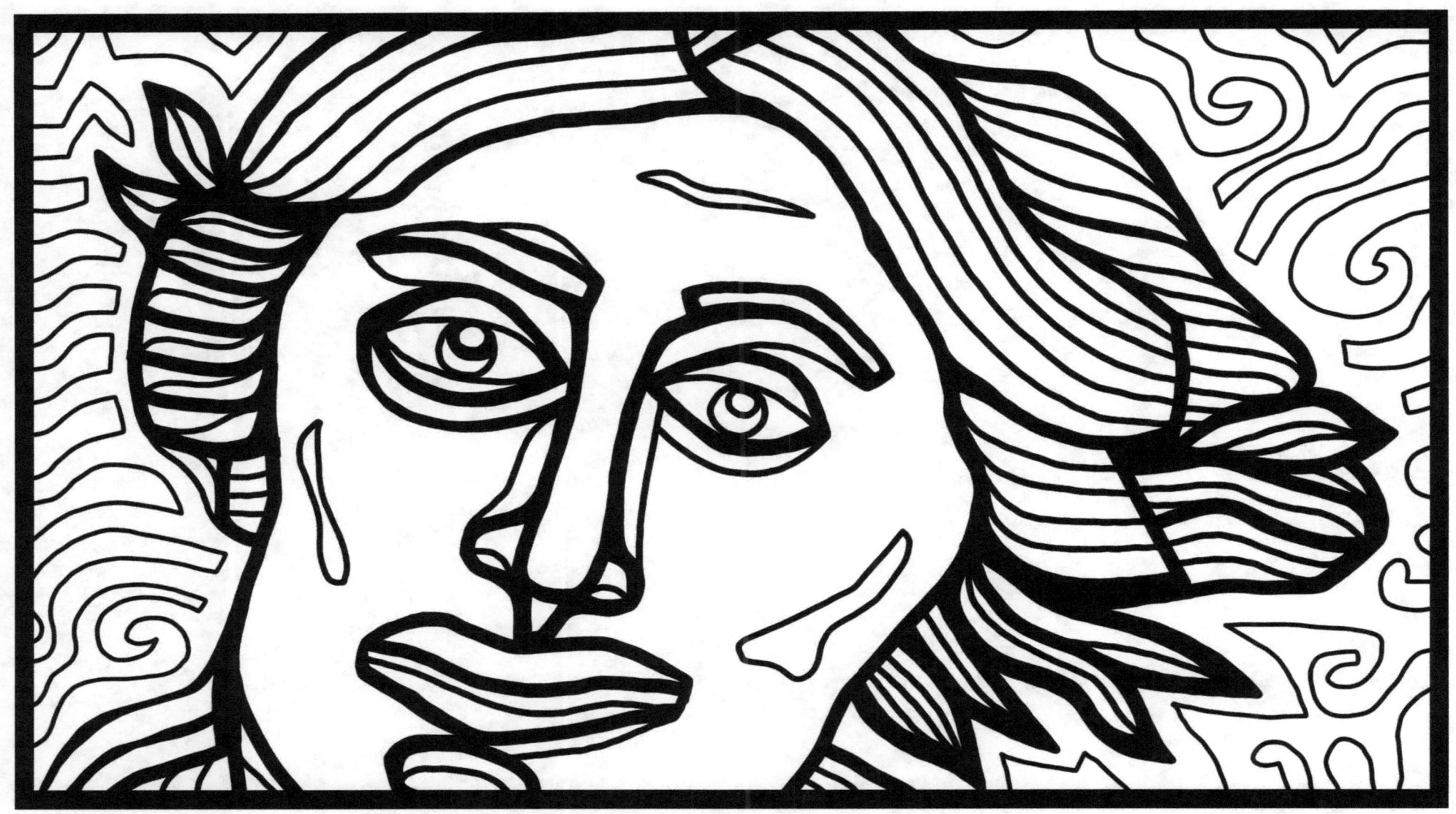

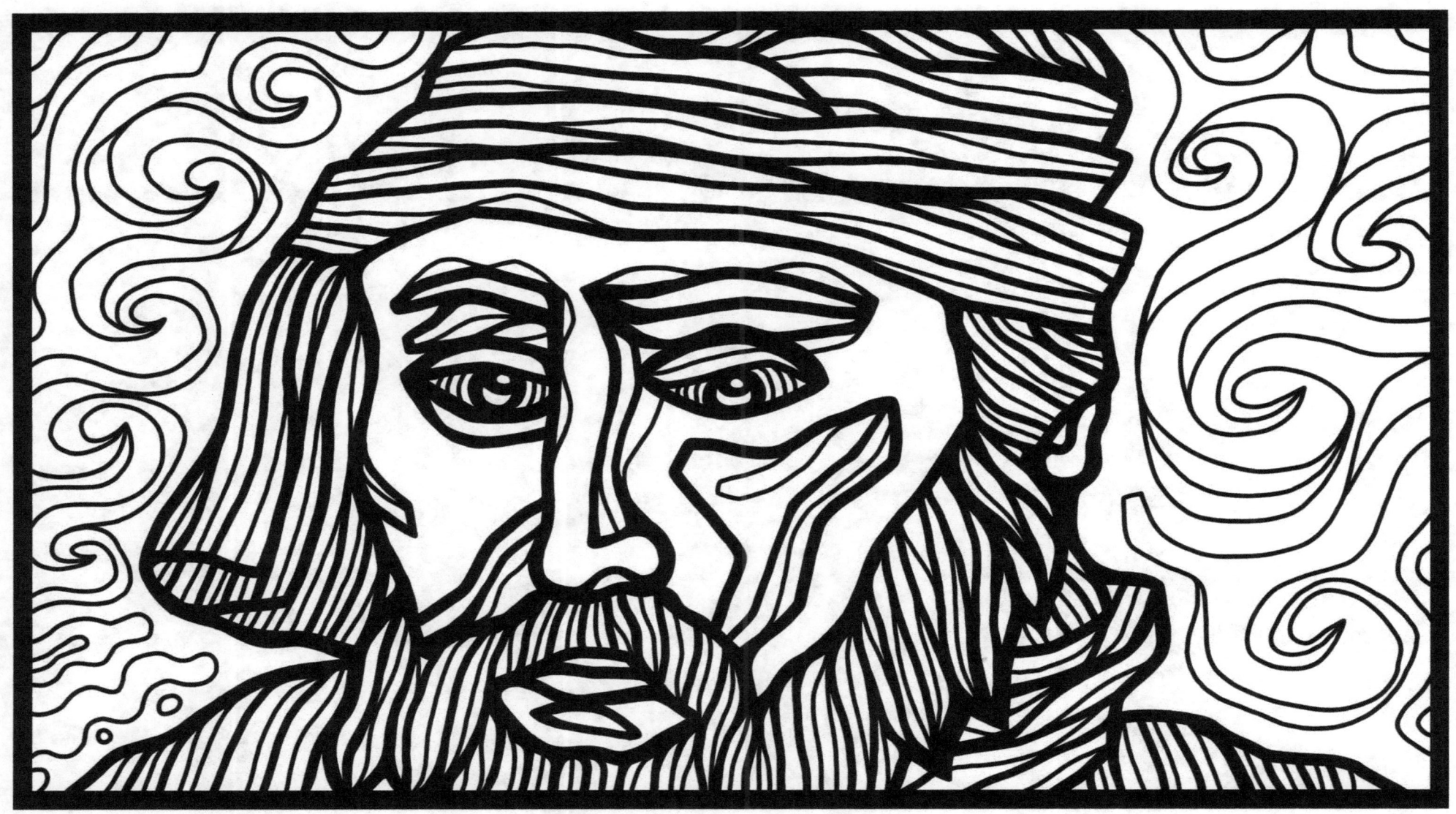

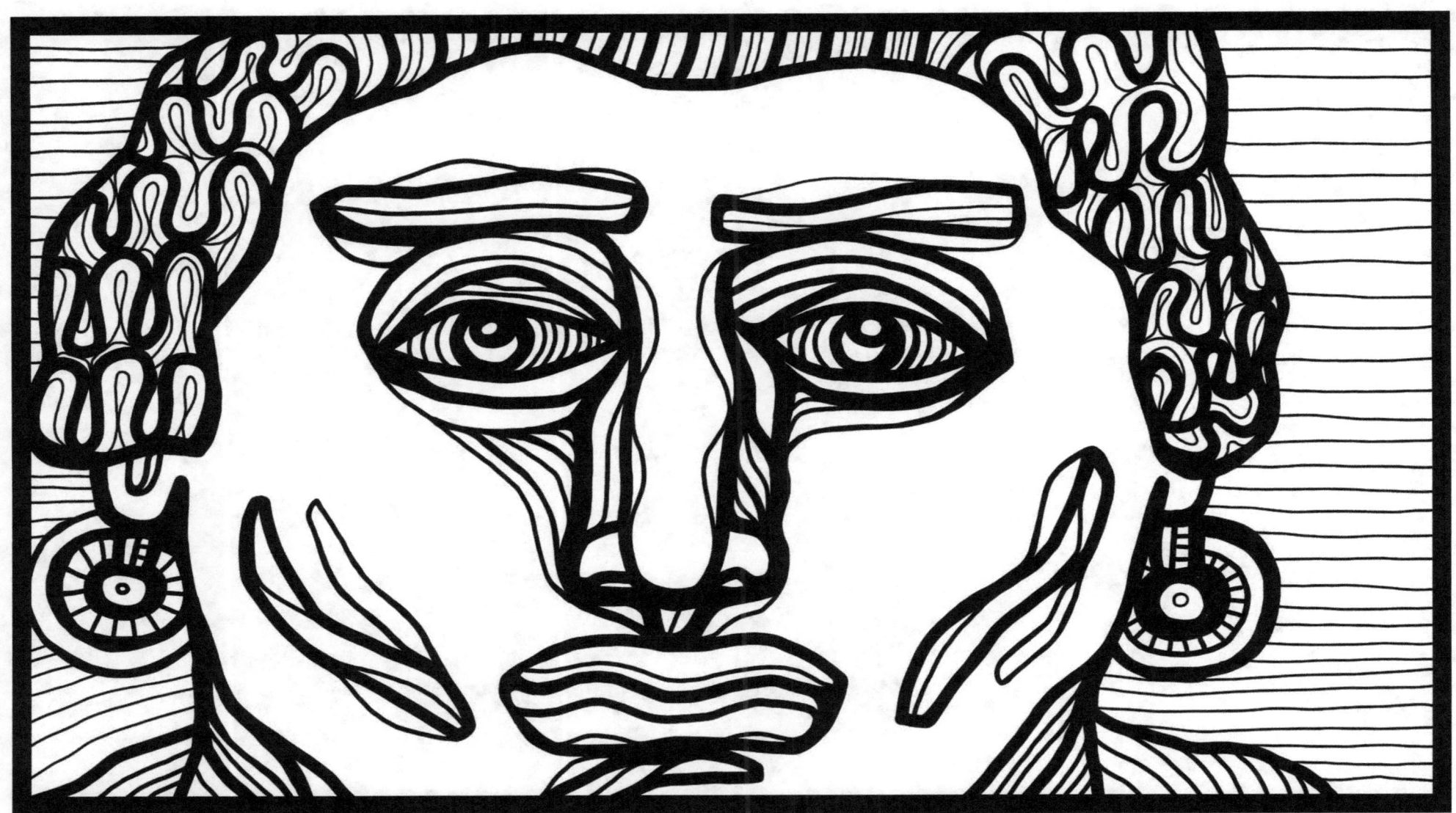

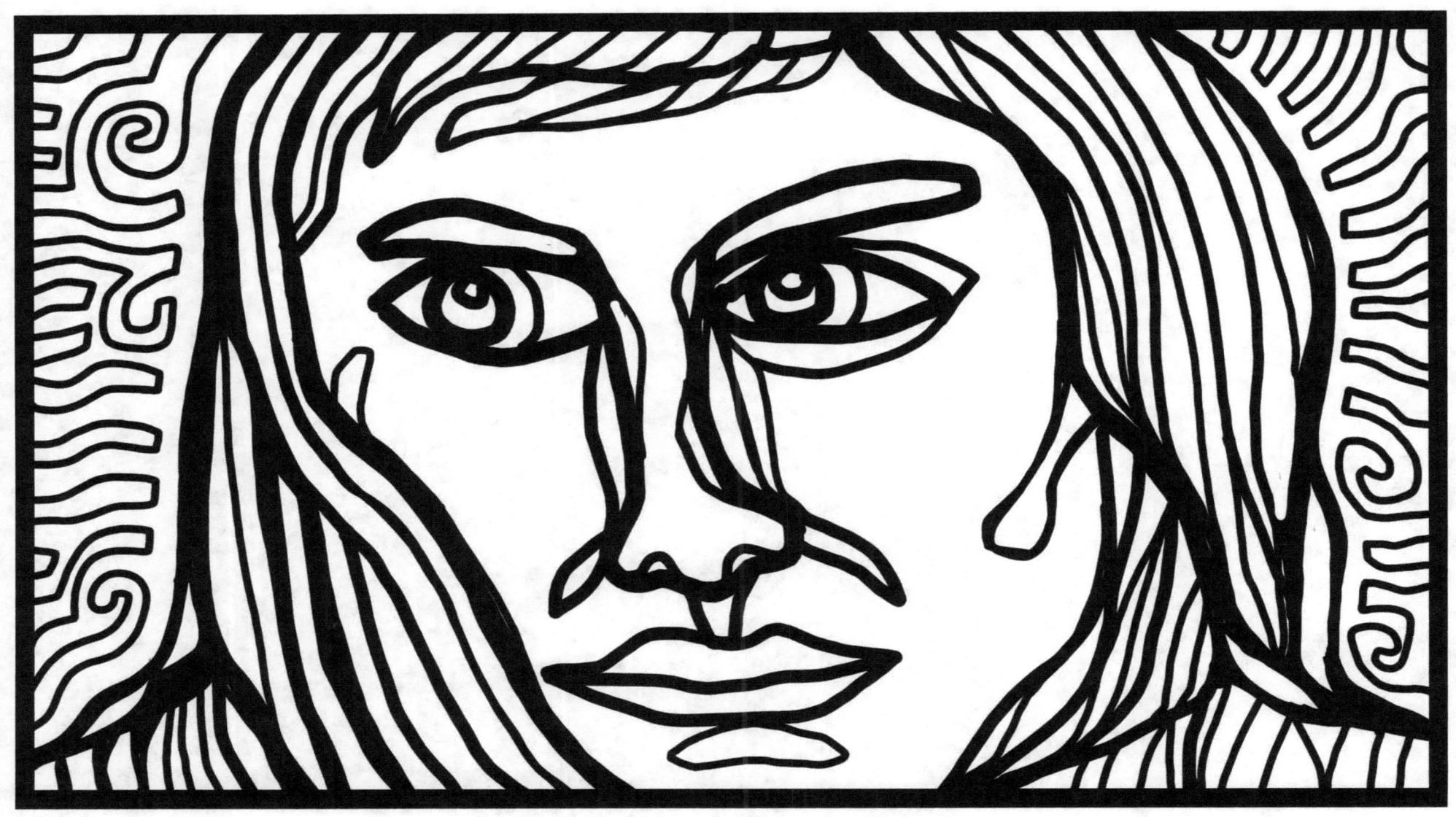

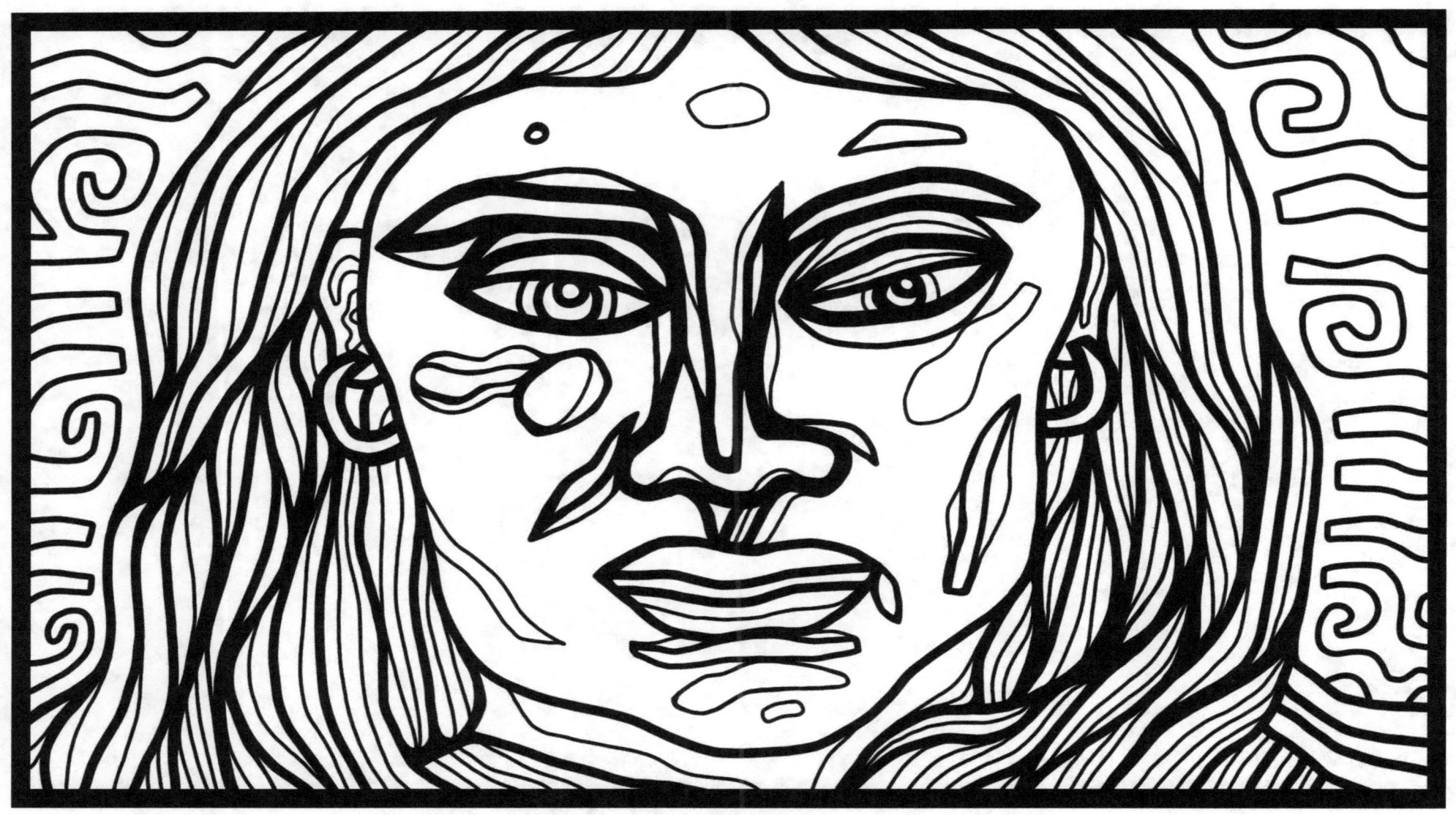

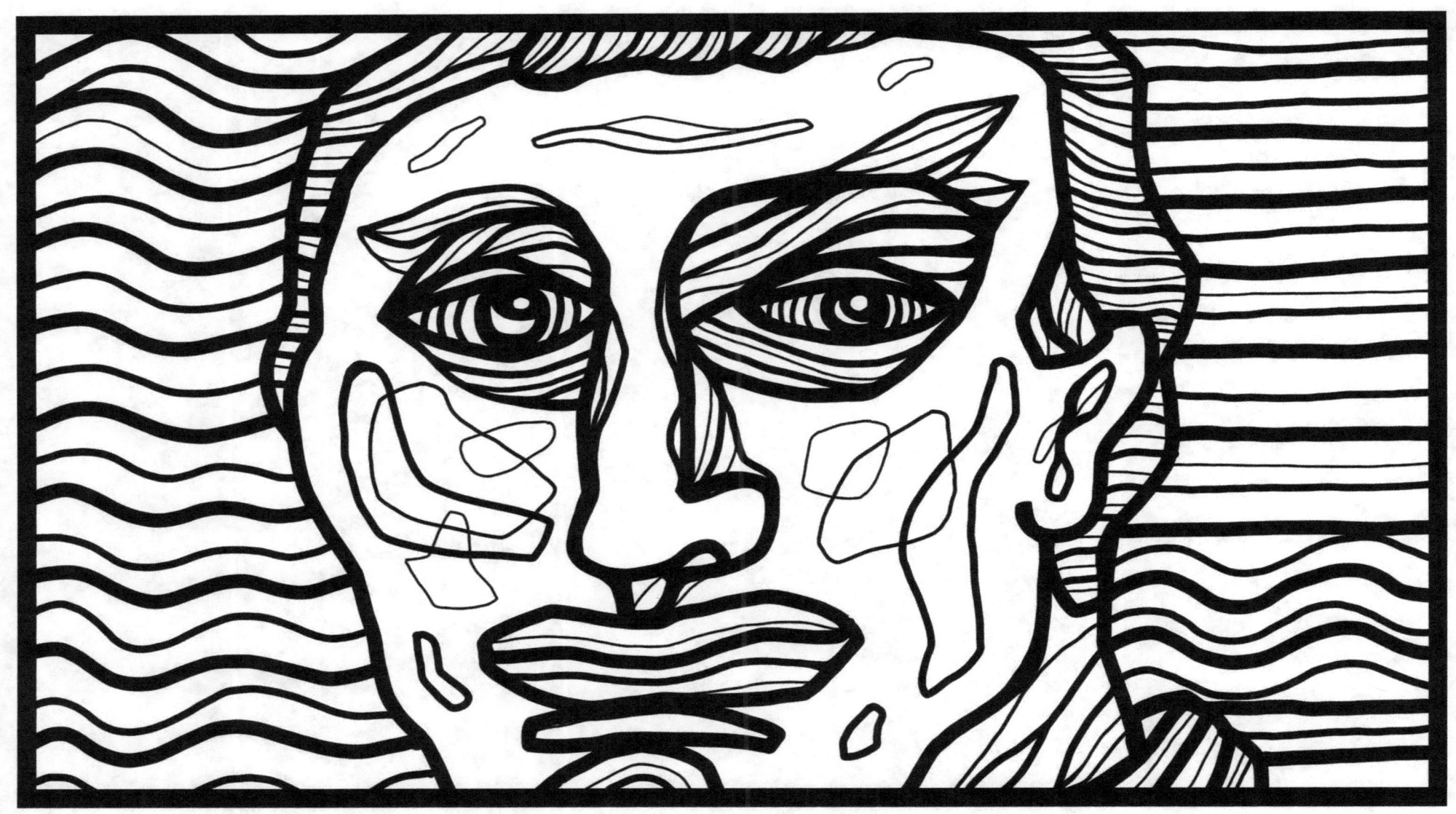

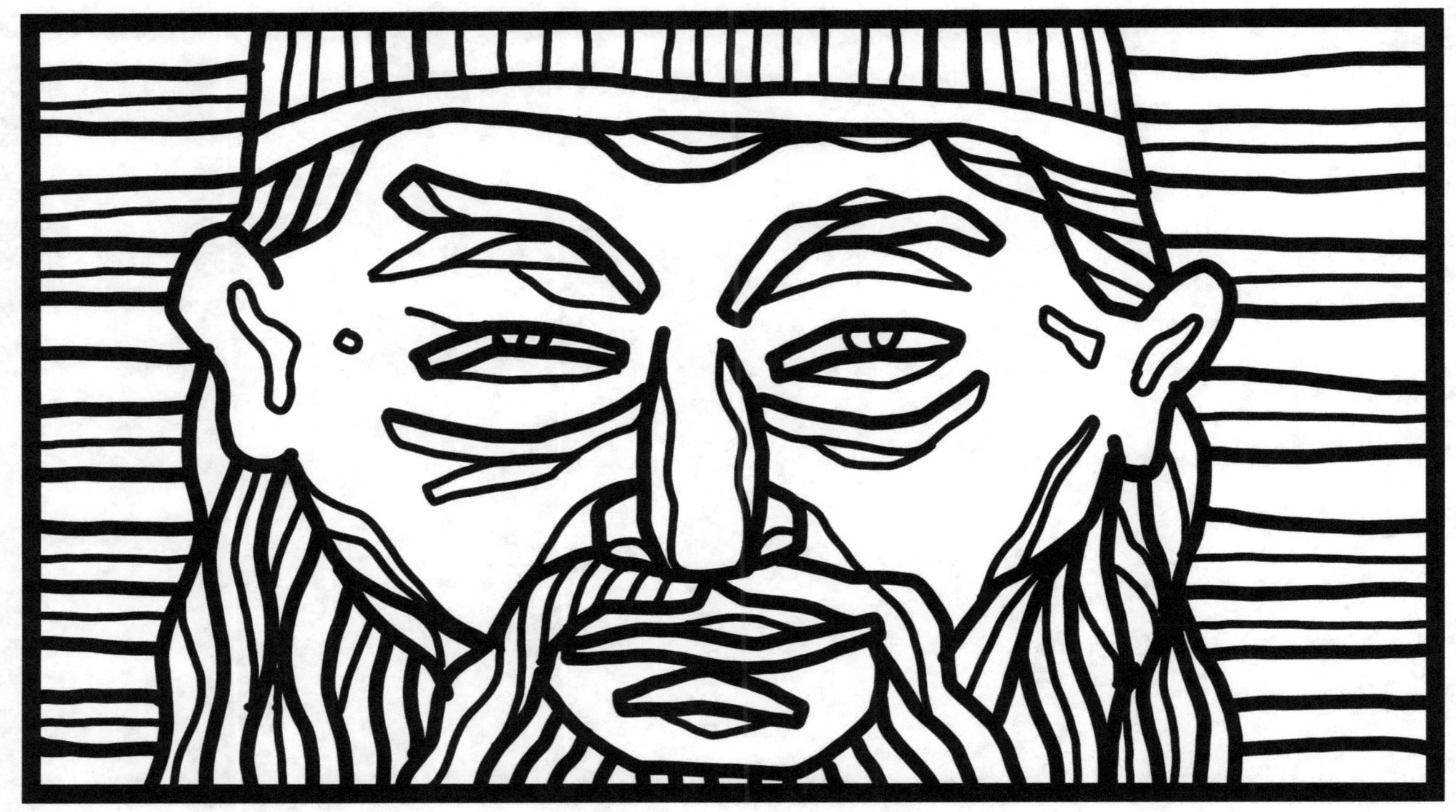

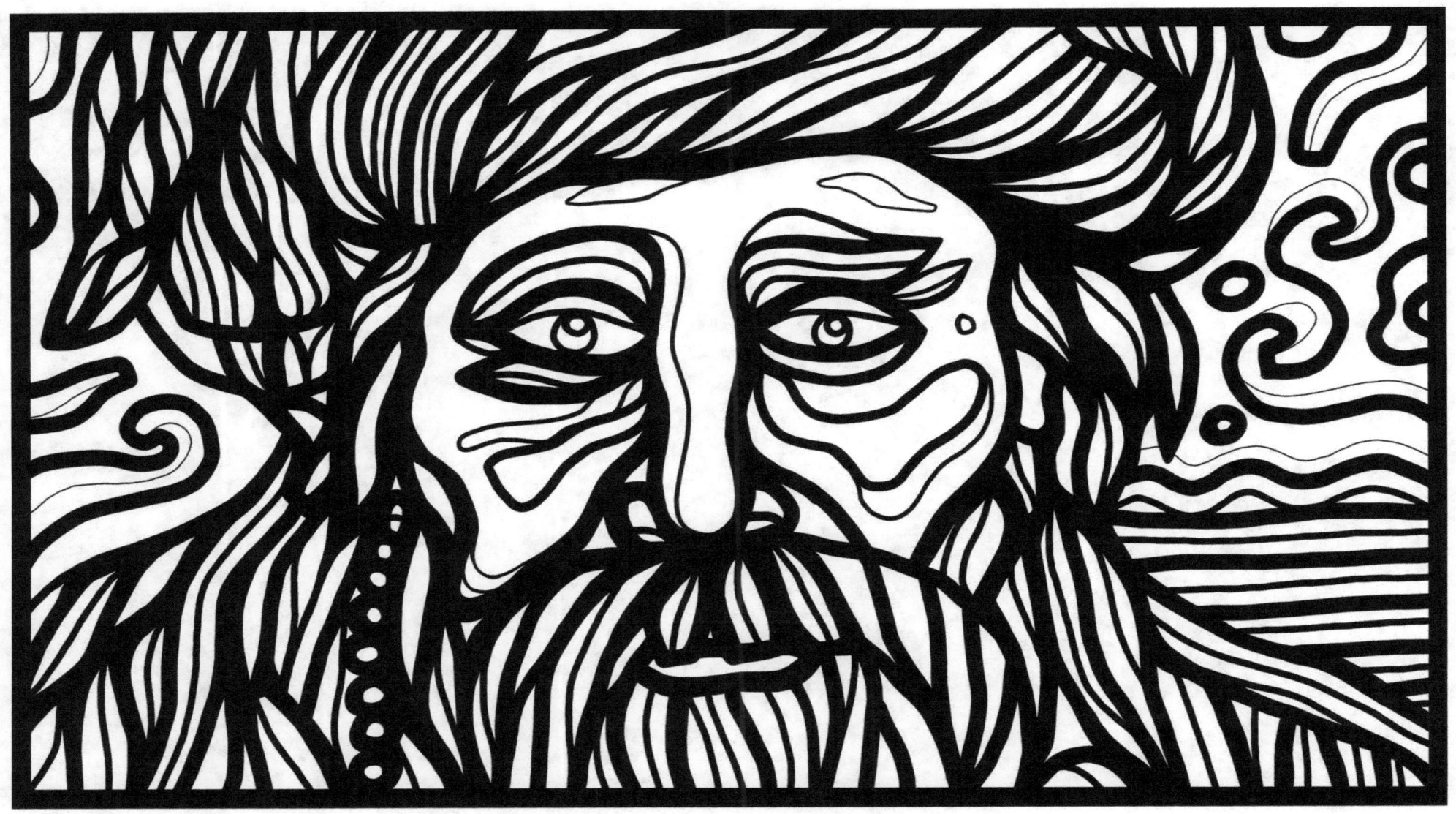

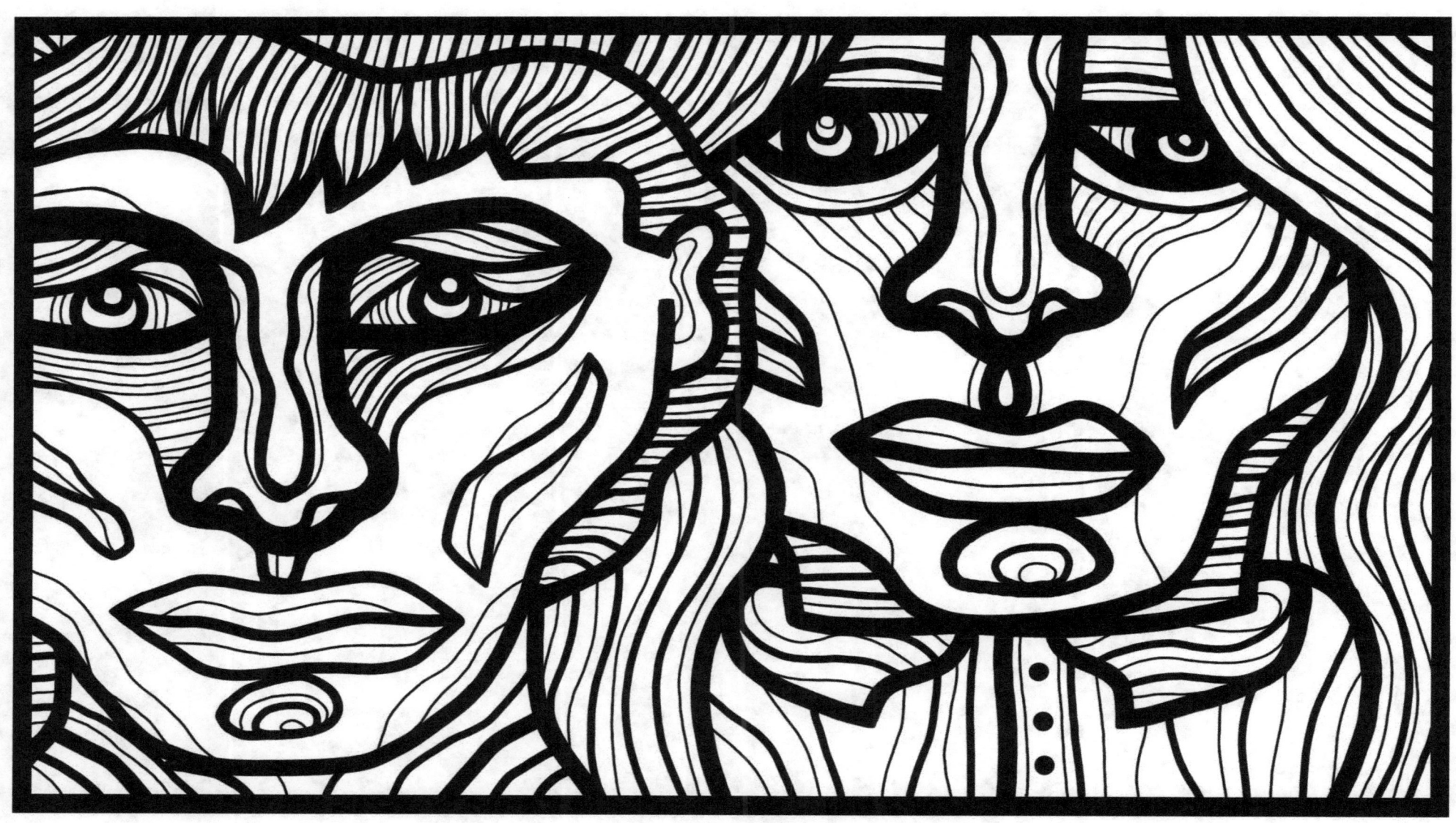

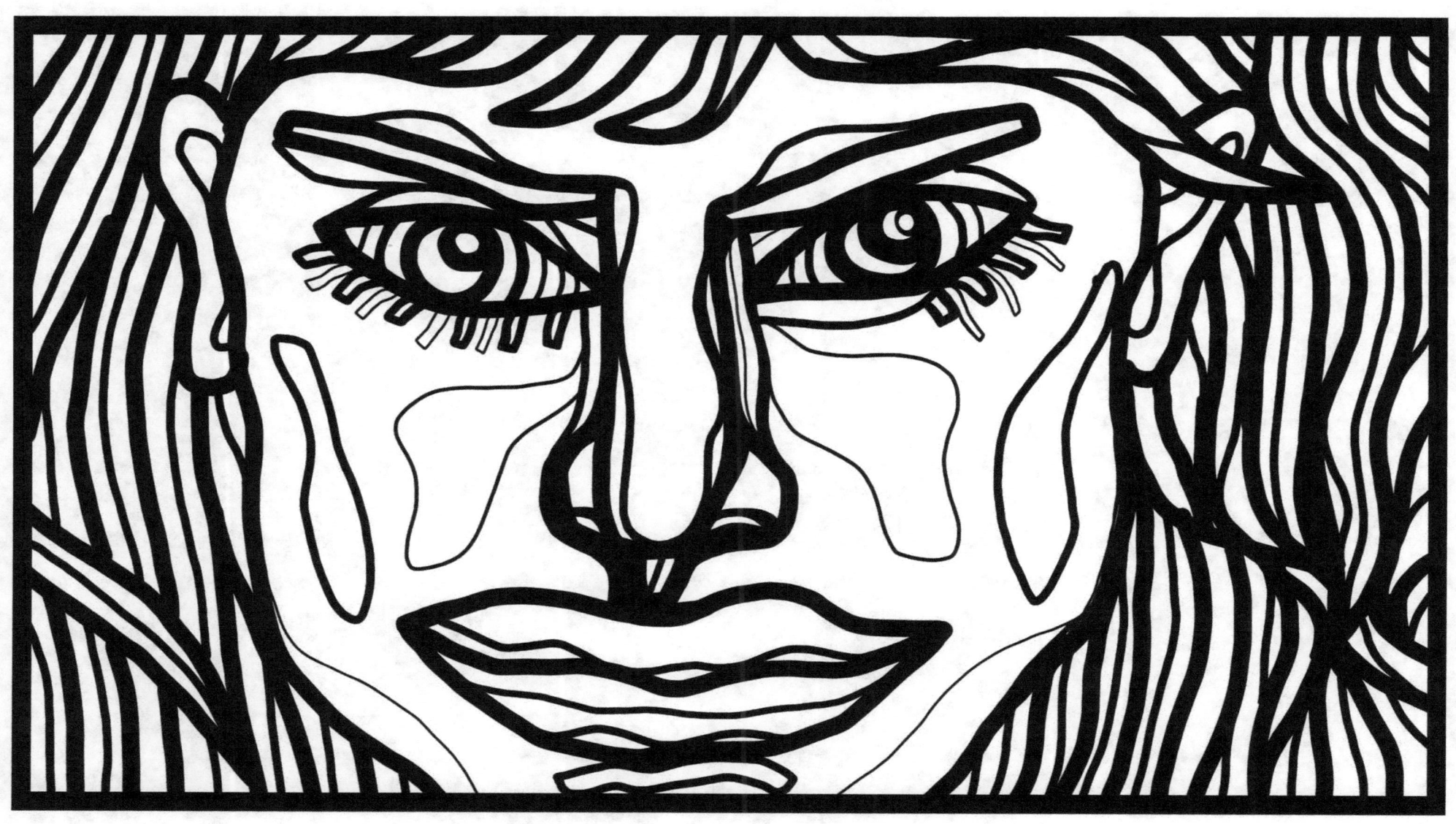

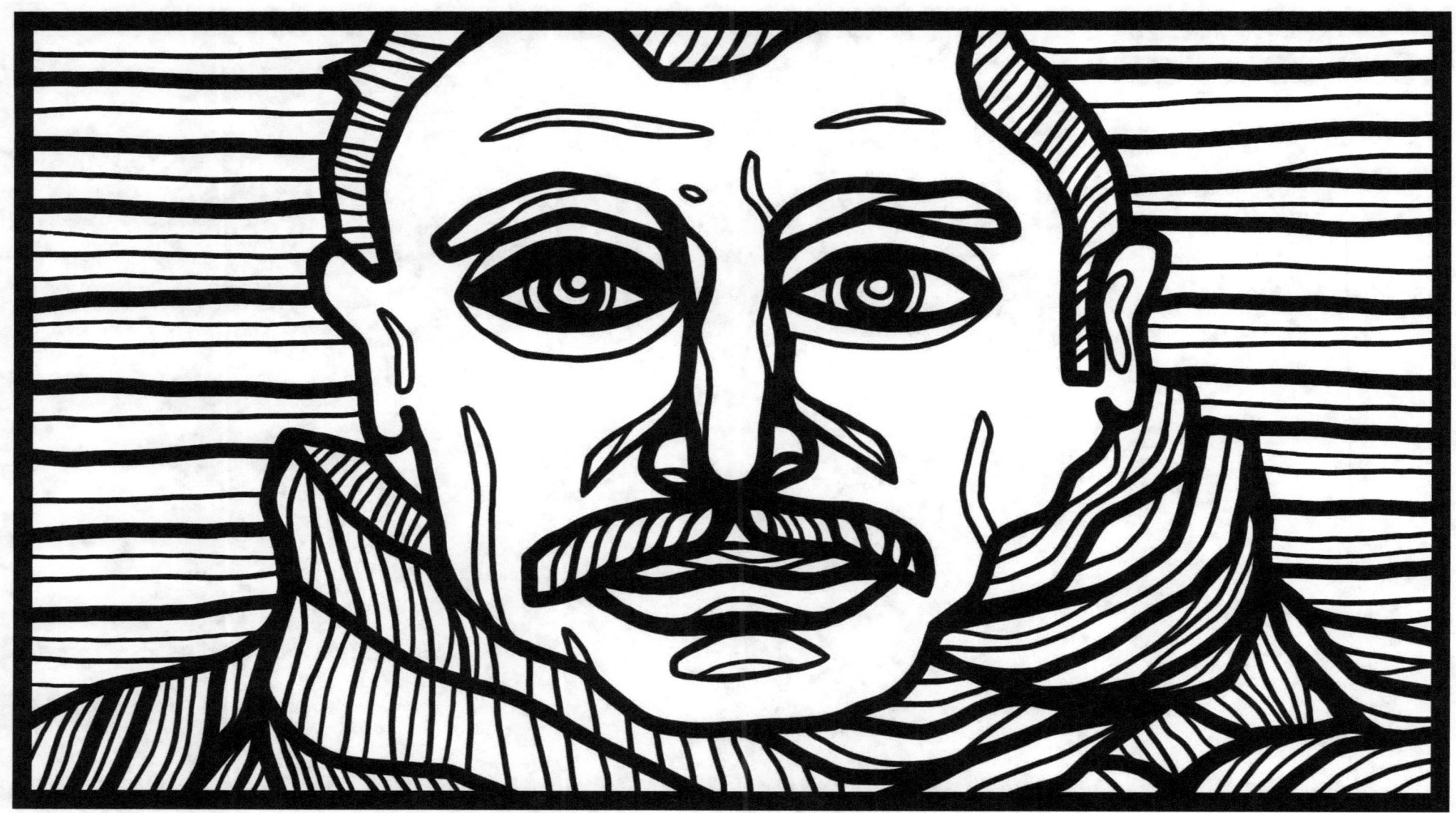

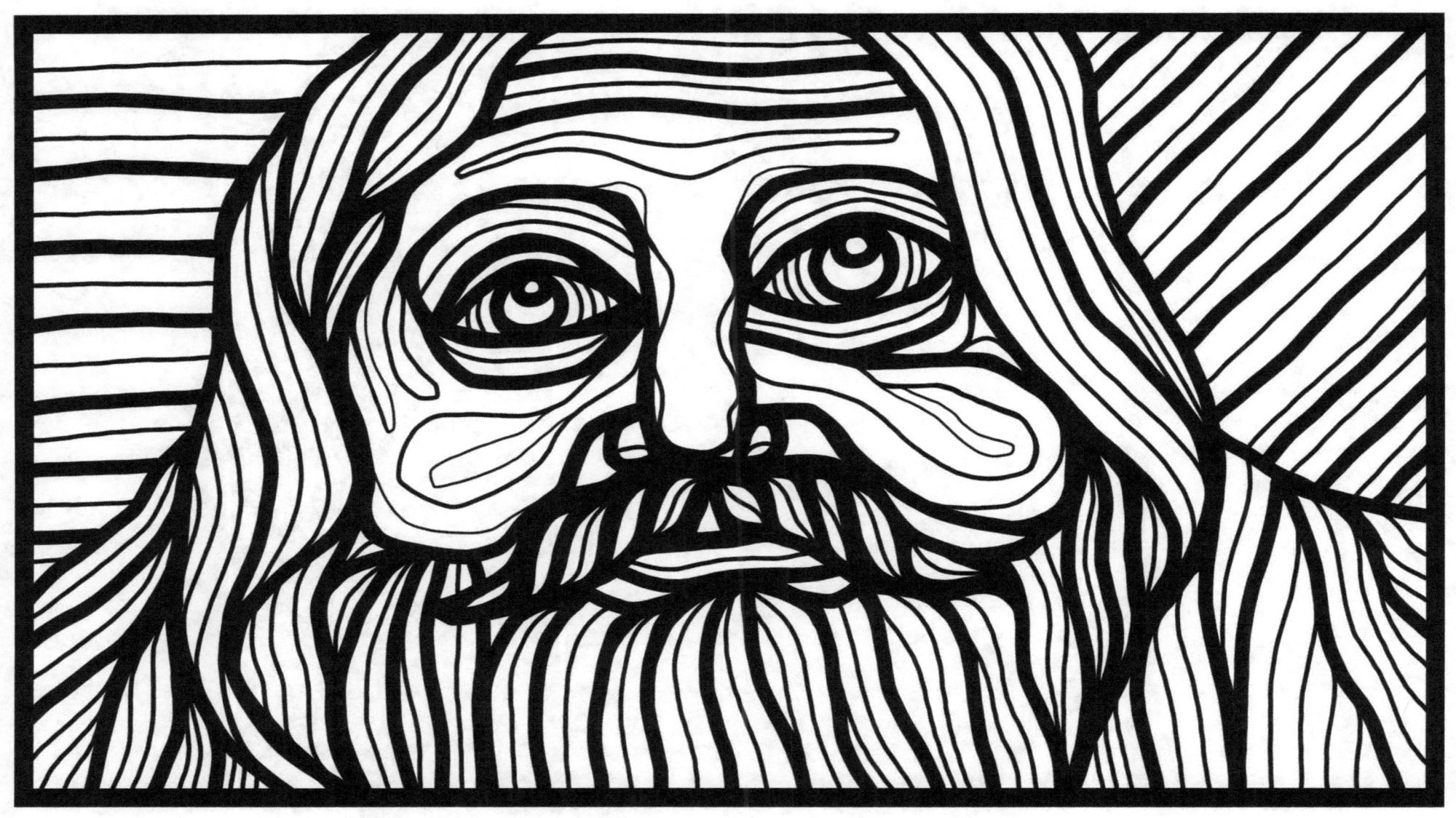

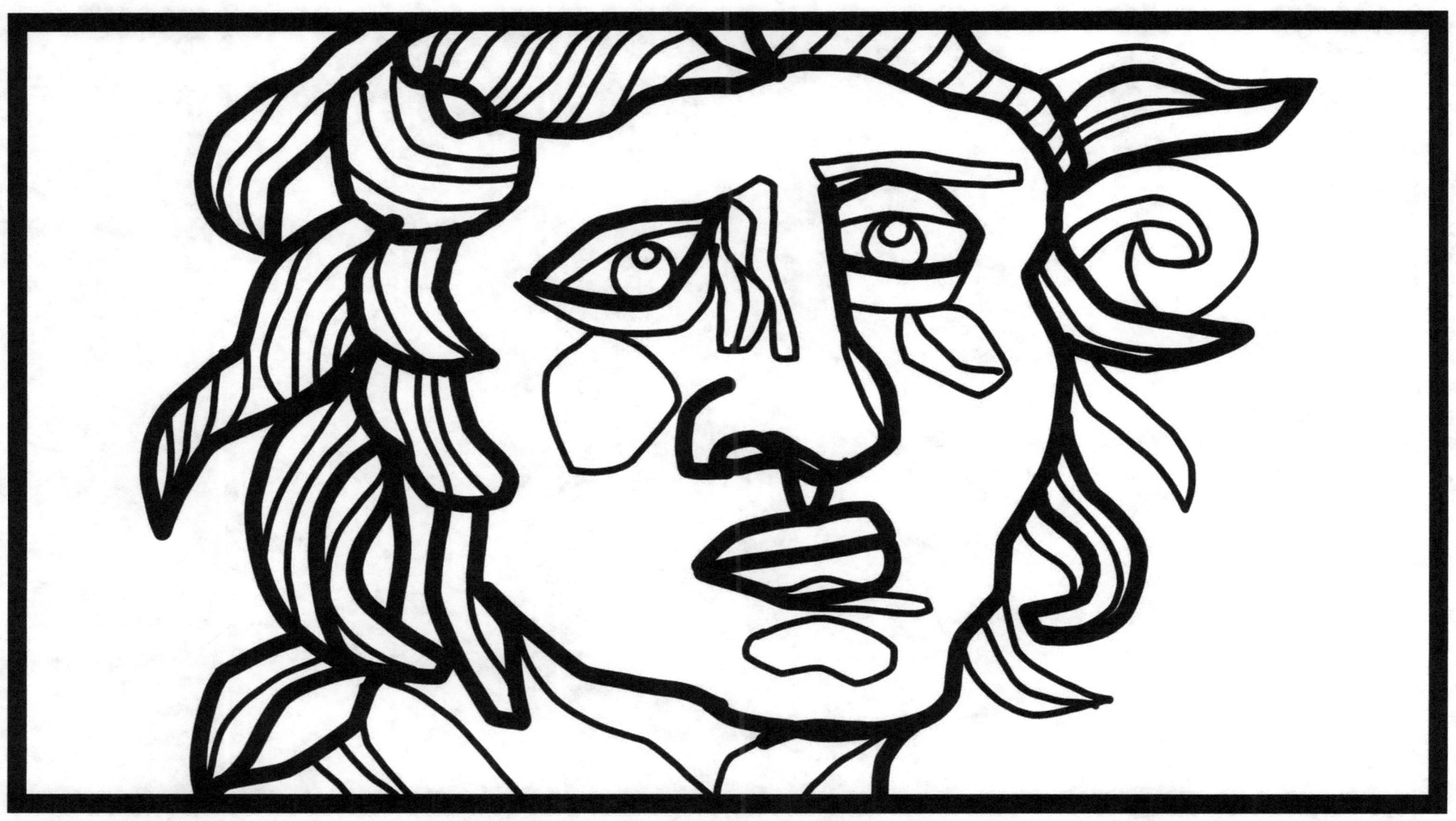

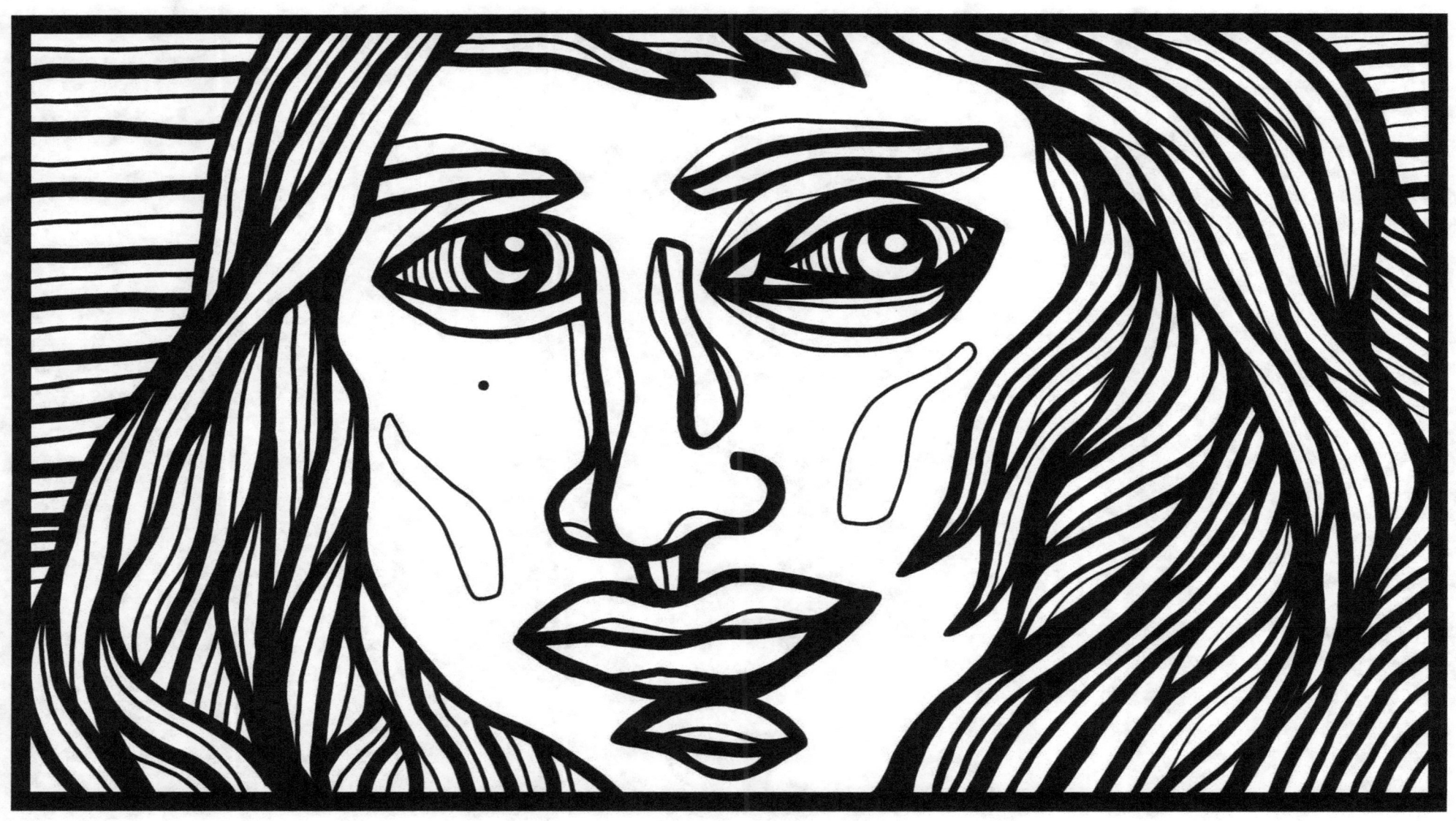

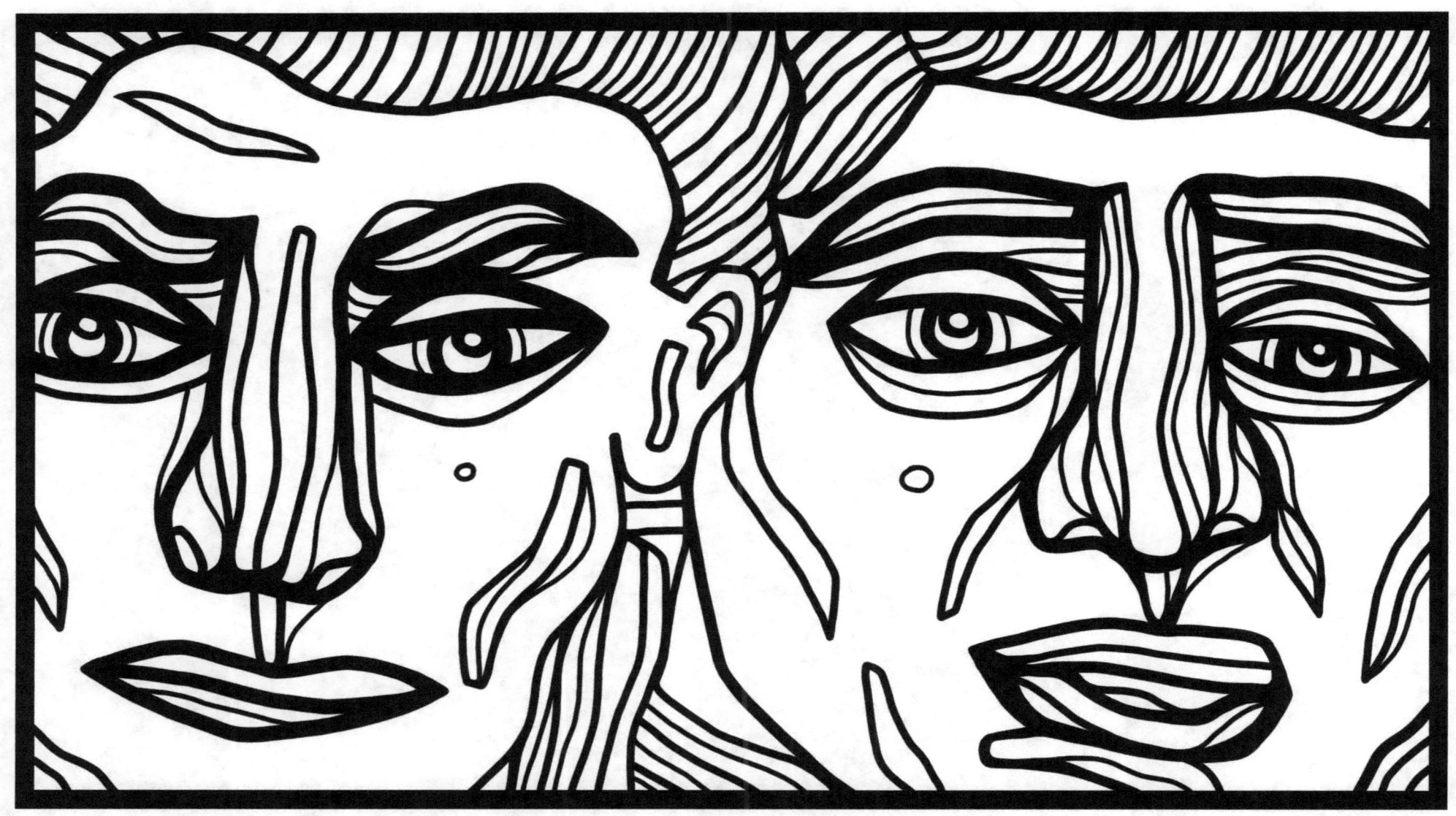

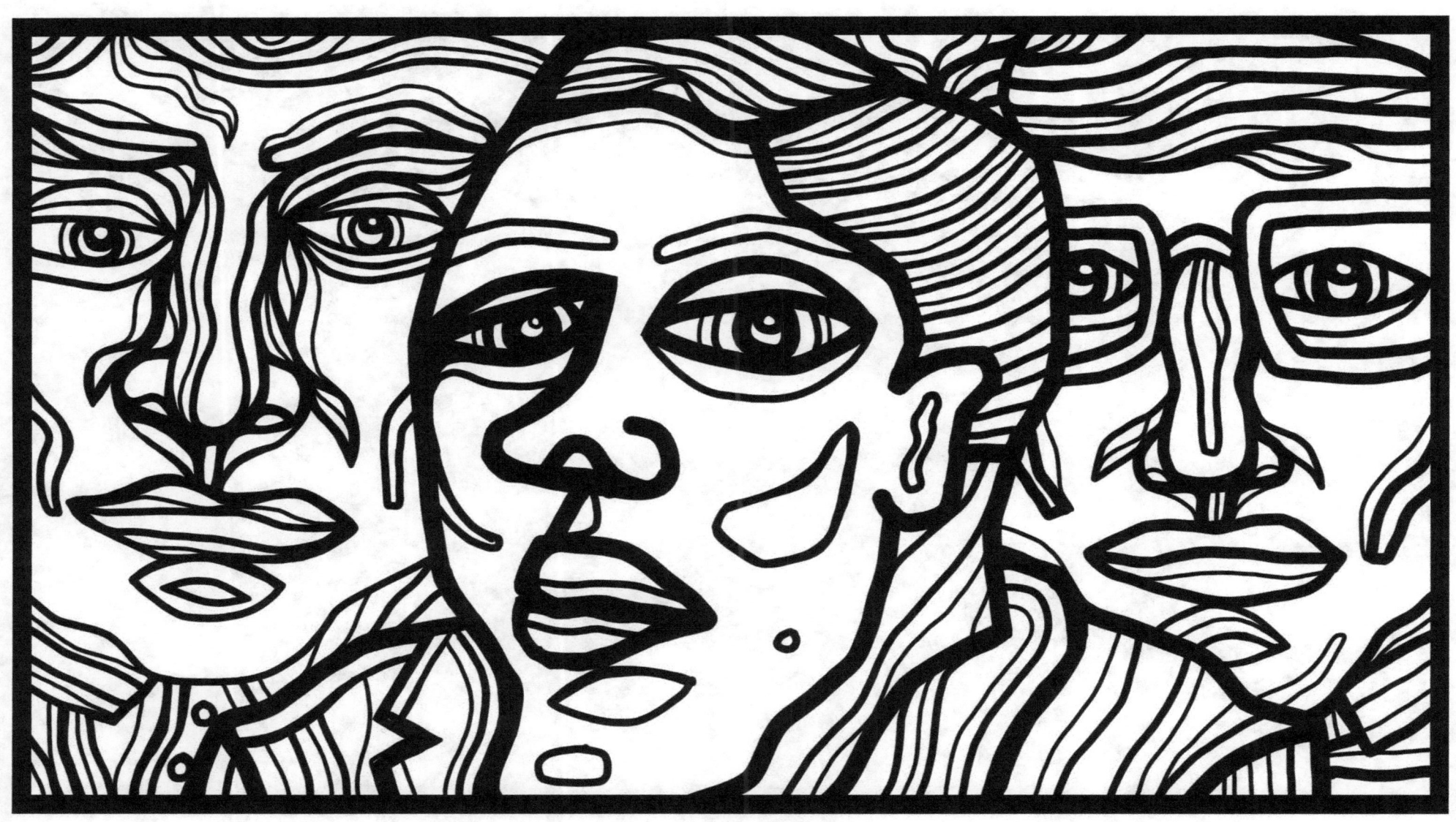

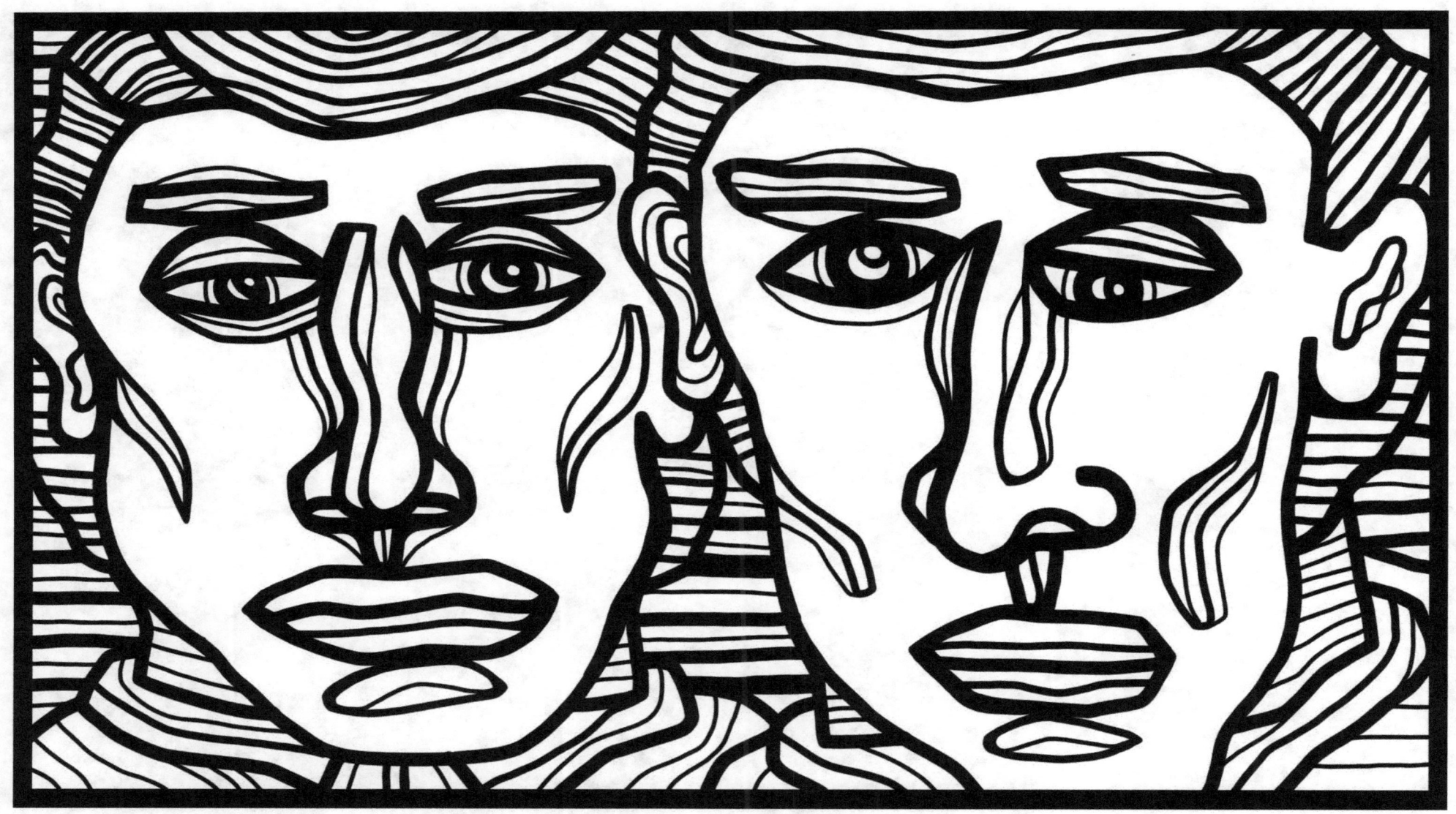

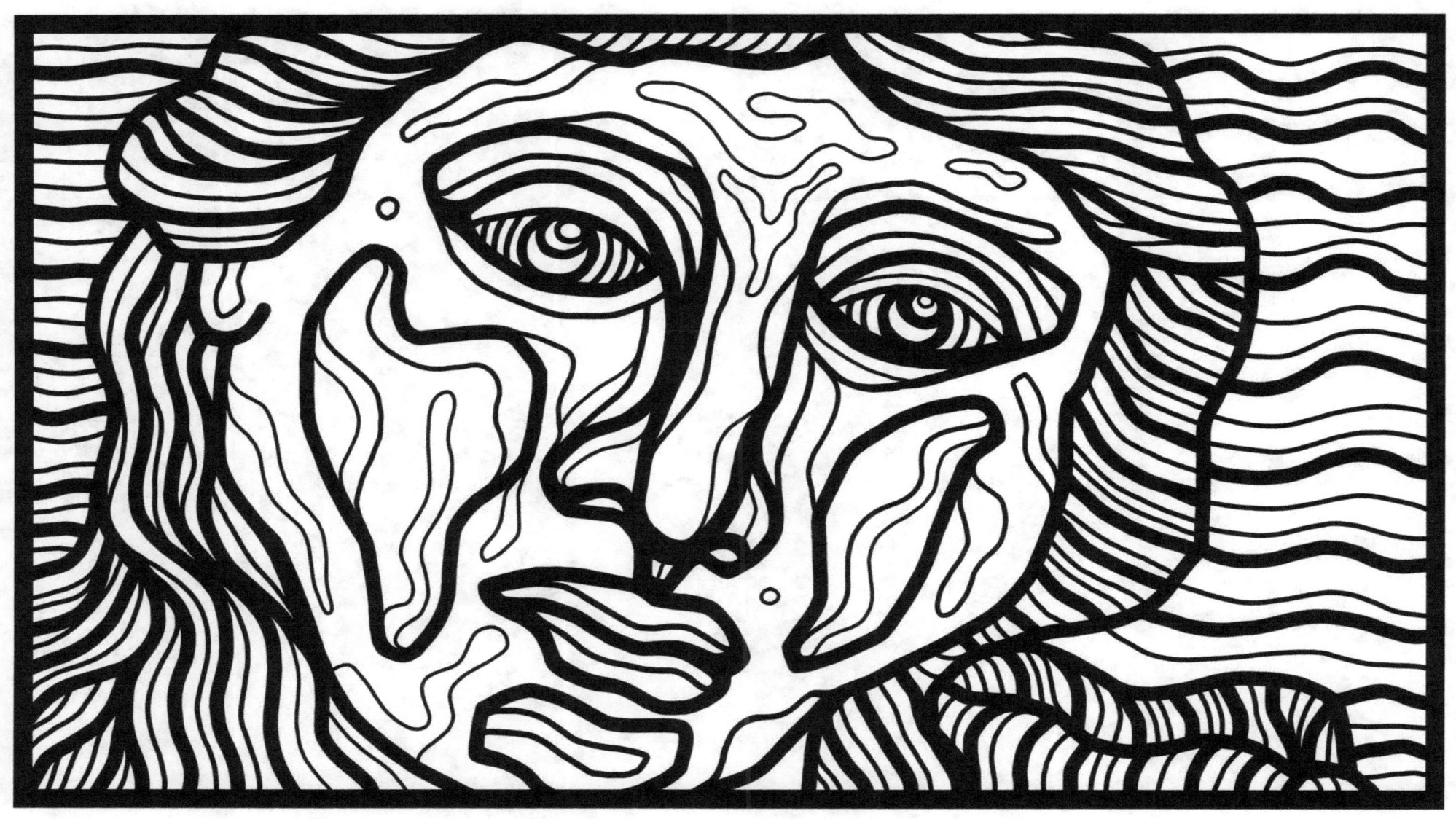

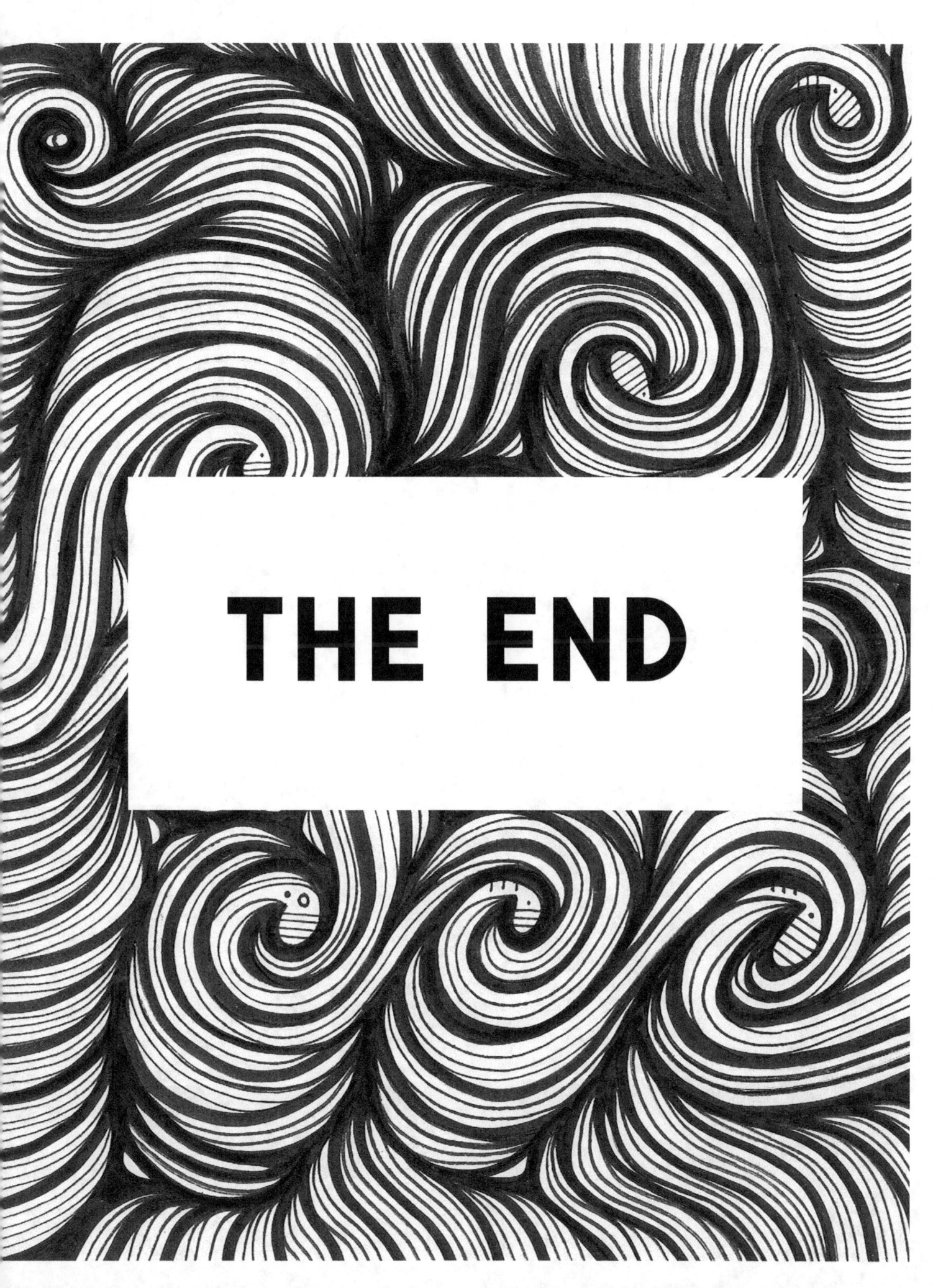

THE END

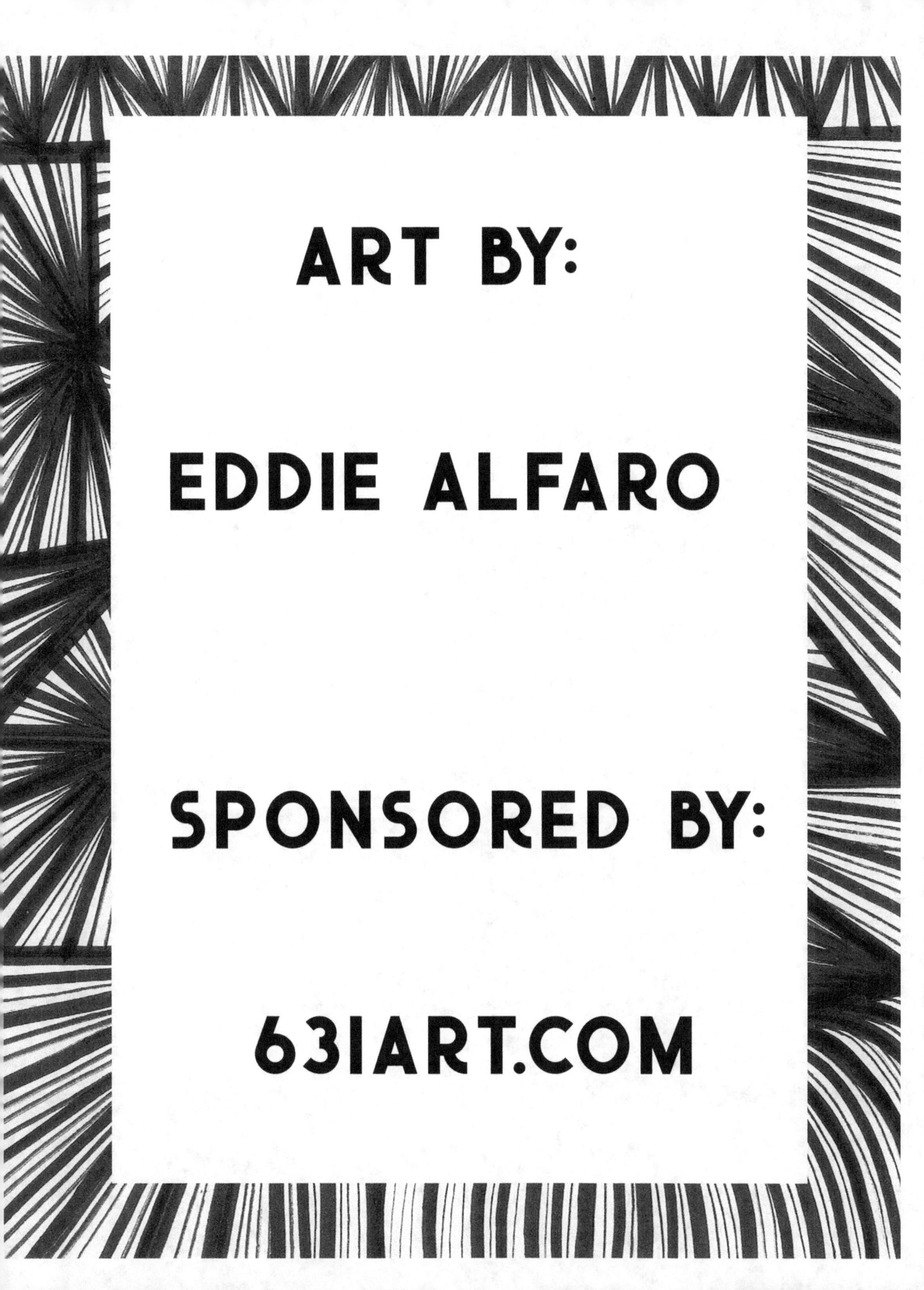

ART BY:

EDDIE ALFARO

SPONSORED BY:

631ART.COM

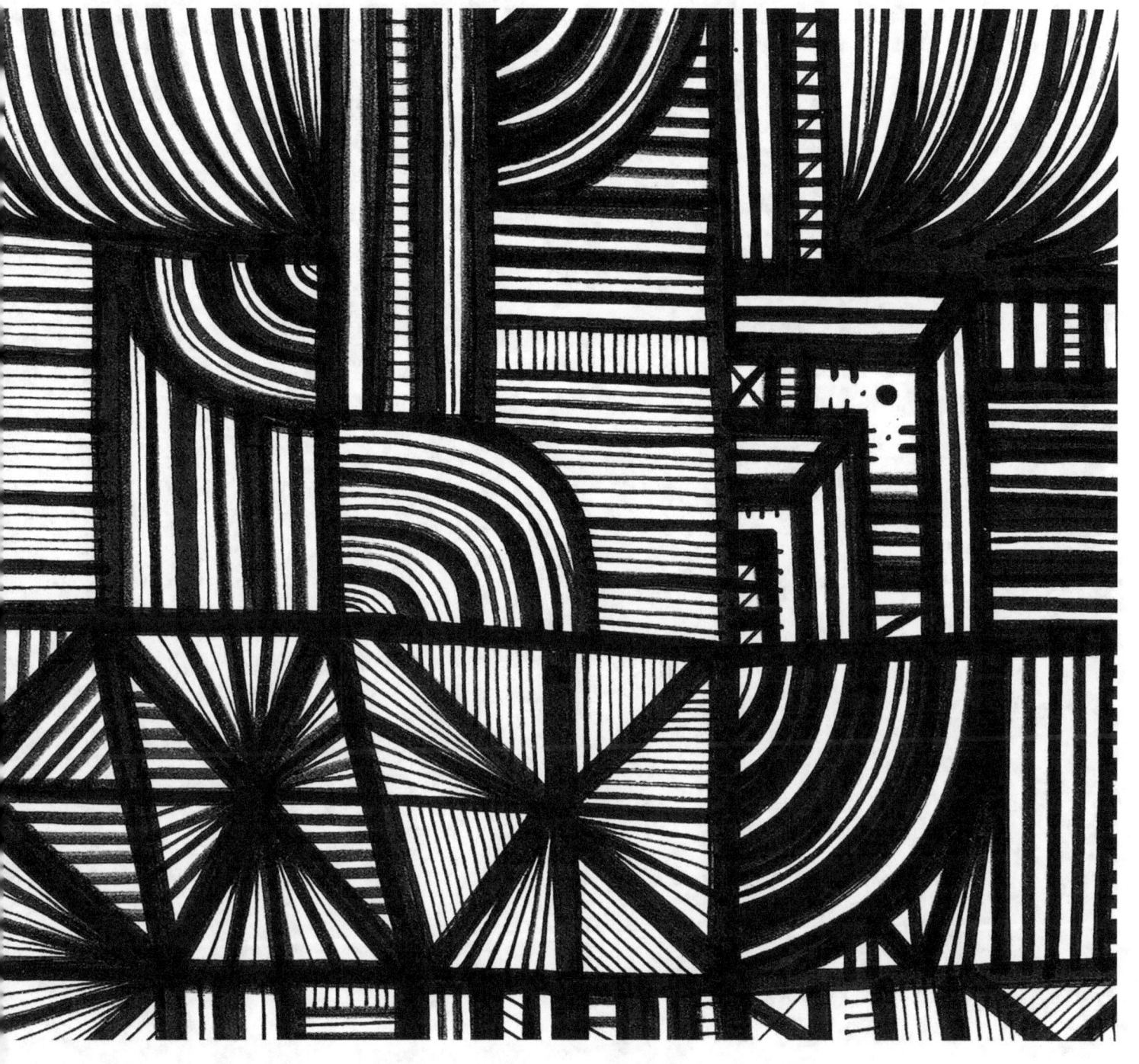

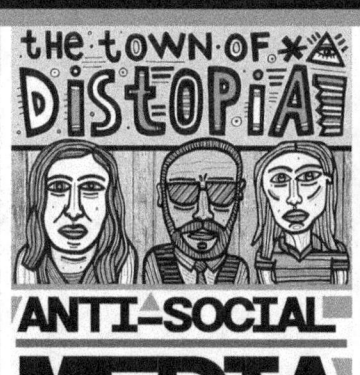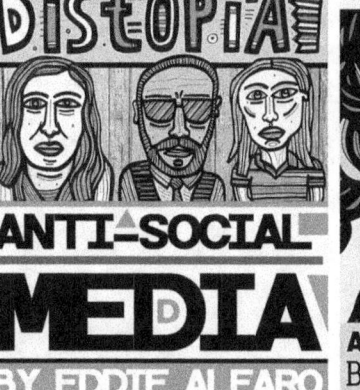
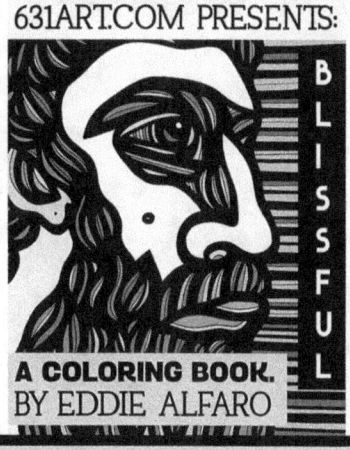
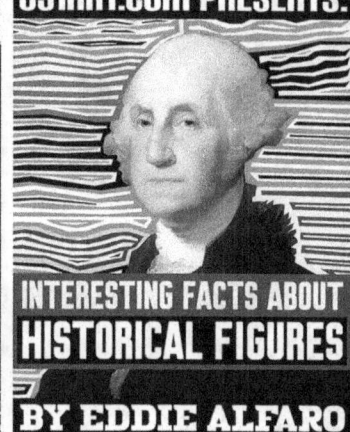
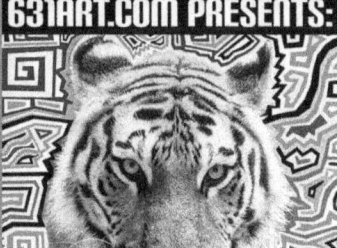
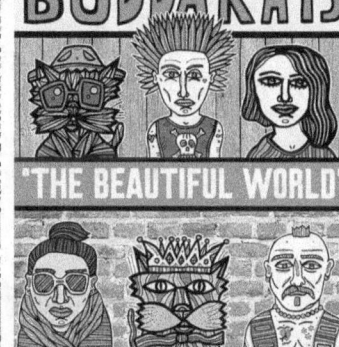
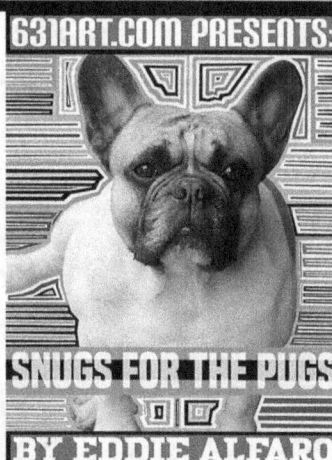
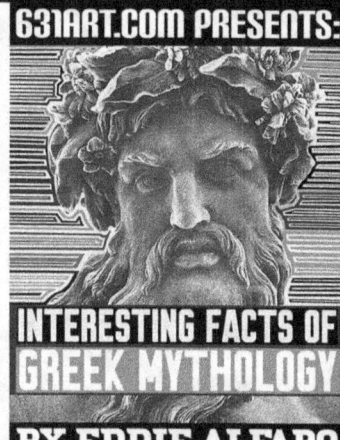
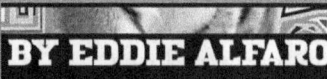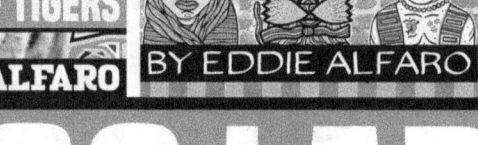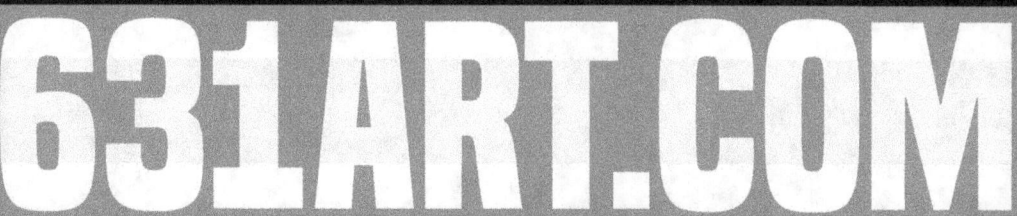
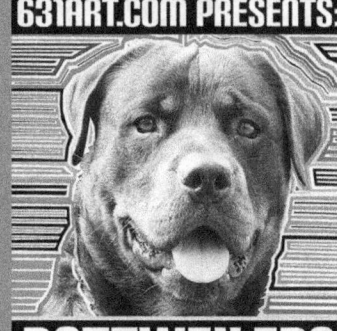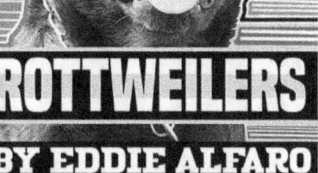
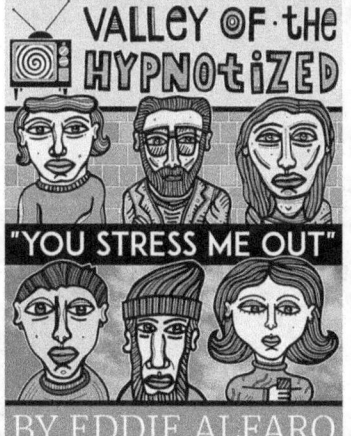
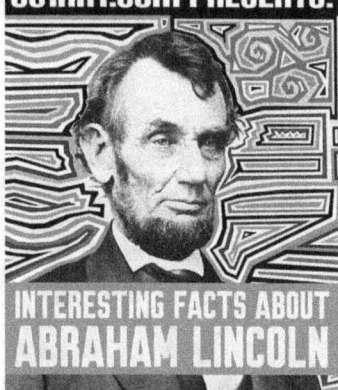
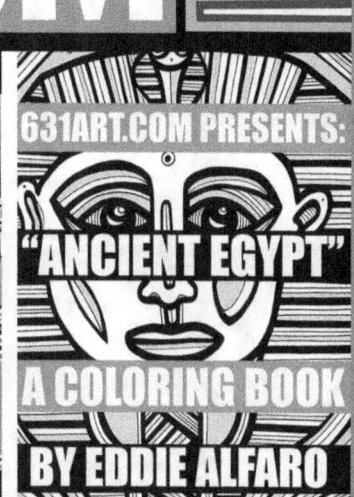

www.ingramcontent.com/pod-product-compliance
Lightning Source LLC
Chambersburg PA
CBHW081627220526
45468CB00009B/2335